1
N

OF 1991

JOCELYN A. BEARD has edited <u>The Best Men's Stage Monologues of 1990</u>, <u>The Best Women's Stage Monologues of 1990</u>, <u>One Hundred Men's Stage Monologues from the 1980's</u>, <u>One Hundred Women's Stage Monologues from the 1980's</u>, and has co-edited <u>The Best Stage Scenes for Men from the 1980's</u> and <u>The Best Stage Scenes for Women from the 1980's</u>.

DAVID FRANK is the Artistic Director of the American Players Theater in Spring Green, Wisconsin.

i

Smith and Kraus *Books For Actors*
THE MONOLOGUE SERIES
> The Best Men's / Women's Stage Monologues of 1994
> The Best Men's / Women's Stage Monologues of 1993
> The Best Men's / Women's Stage Monologues of 1992
> The Best Men's / Women's Stage Monologues of 1991
> The Best Men's / Women's Stage Monologues of 1990
> One Hundred Men's / Women's Stage Monologues from the 1980's
> 2 Minutes and Under: Character Monologues for Actors
> Street Talk: Character Monologues for Actors
> Uptown: Character Monologues for Actors
> Ice Babies in Oz: Character Monologues for Actors
> Monologues from Contemporary Literature: Volume I
> Monologues from Classic Plays
> 100 Great Monologues from the Renaissance Theatre
> 100 Great Monologues from the Neo-Classical Theatre
> 100 Great Monologues from the 19th C. Romantic and Realistic Theatres

FESTIVAL MONOLOGUE SERIES
> The Great Monologues from the Humana Festival
> The Great Monologues from the EST Marathon
> The Great Monologues from the Women's Project
> The Great Monologues from the Mark Taper Forum

YOUNG ACTORS SERIES
> Great Scenes and Monologues for Children
> New Plays from A.C.T.'s Young Conservatory
> Great Scenes for Young Actors from the Stage
> Great Monologues for Young Actors
> Multicultural Monologues for Young Actors
> Multicultural Scenes for Young Actors

SCENE STUDY SERIES
> Scenes From Classic Plays 468 B.C. to 1960 A.D.
> The Best Stage Scenes of 1995
> The Best Stage Scenes of 1994
> The Best Stage Scenes of 1993
> The Best Stage Scenes of 1992
> The Best Stage Scenes for Men / Women from the 1980's

CONTEMPORARY PLAYWRIGHTS SERIES
> Christopher Durang Vol. I: 27 Short Plays
> Jane Martin Vol. I: Collected Plays
> Romulus Linney: 17 Short Plays
> Eric Overmyer: Collected Plays
> Lanford Wilson: 21 Short Plays
> Lanford Wilson Vol. II: Early Plays
> William Mastrosimone: Collected Plays
> Horton Foote: 4 New Plays
> Israel Horovitz: 16 Short Plays
> Israel Horovitz: New England Blue, 4 Plays of Working Class Life
> Terrence McNally: 15 Short Plays
> Humana Festival '93: The Complete Plays
> Humana Festival '94: The Complete Plays
> Humana Festival '95: The Complete Plays
> Women Playwrights: The Best Plays of 1992
> Women Playwrights: The Best Plays of 1993
> Women Playwrights: The Best Plays of 1994

CAREER DEVELOPMENT SERIES
> The Job Book: 100 Acting Jobs for Actors
> How to Audition for the Musical Theatre
> The Camera Smart Actor
> The Sanford Meisner Approach
> The Actor's Chekhov
> Kiss and Tell: Restoration Scenes, Monologues, & History
> Cold Readings: Some Do's and Don'ts for Actors at Auditions

If you require pre-publication information about upcoming Smith and Kraus books, you may receive our semi-annual catalogue, free of charge, by sending your name and address to *Smith and Kraus Catalogue, P.O. Box 127, One Main Street, Lyme, NH 03768. Or call us at (800) 895-4331, fax (603) 795-4427.*

THE BEST
MEN'S STAGE
MONOLOGUES
OF 1991

Edited By
Jocelyn A. Beard

SK
A Smith and Kraus Book

A Smith and Kraus Book
Published by Smith and Kraus, Inc.

Cover and text design by Jeannette Champagne

Manufactured in the United States of America

First Edition: January 1992
10 9 8 7 6 5 4 3 2

Publisher's Cataloging in Publication
(Prepared by Quality Books Inc.)

The best men's stage monologues of 1991/Jocelyn A. Beard.
p. cm.
Includes bibliographical references.
ISBN 1-880399-02-4

1. Monologues. 2. Acting. I. Beard, Jocelyn A.
PN4307.M6   808.8245
                              91-66287

Smith and Kraus, Inc.
Main Street, P.O. Box 10, Newbury, Vermont 05051
(802) 866-5423

ACKNOWLEDGMENTS

Grateful thanks to the playwrights and their agents. Jocelyn A. Beard would also like to thank Kevin Kitowski for his love and support.

CONTENTS

CONTENTS

CONTENTS

FOREWORD

If 1991 is any indication, the 90's are going to be rich years for theater. With the growing pains of the last three decades finally behind us, the final years of this millennium promise to provide actors with roles that will challenge as well as break new theatrical ground. 1991 saw the continuing rise of the repertory theater as a definitive source of fresh and innovative work, presenting actors with unique opportunities to tackle roles on the cutting edge of their art.

The plays of 1991 introduced us to men's characters of substance. Alvin, of Wil Calhoun's *The Balcony Scene* is an agoraphobic writer terrified to leave the safe confines of his apartment. In Richard Lay's *Sparky's Last Dance*, we meet Hurricane, a man on death row evaluating his life on the eve of his execution. And finally, in David Hirson's brilliant *La Bête*, we are delighted by the word-play of Elomire, a 17th century actor/playwright who is threatened by the encroachment of mediocrity into his art.

Crack, gay relationships, racial conflict, serial killers, missile silos, homelessness, the handicapped, police corruption, stand-up comedy and sexual dysfunction are just some of the topics explored in the monologues in this book; and it is my hope that you will take advantage of this cornucopia by finding within it the perfect monologue.

Break that leg!

—Jocelyn A. Beard
Patterson, NY
Winter 1991

xi

INTRODUCTION

I imagine you have already discovered how hard it can be to find good audition material. Take comfort, you're on the right track—you've refused to settle for yet another rendition of Tom's opening monologue from *The Glass Menagerie*. You may even be leafing through this volume a little surreptitiously—as if using it were equivalent to relying on Cliff Notes instead of studying the original material. Don't worry, you can (and should) track down the complete play once you've found a speech that appeals to you. Meanwhile, this intelligent and practical collection can point you to excellent material you would probably have missed and save you many hours of research that can be applied to preparing your audition speeches.

Finding good material for a general audition is hard. The task is all the more daunting, given the critical importance of the general audition as a first step toward landing a role early in one's career. At some point in the future you will probably be invited to read for specific roles directly from the text; and when your work is even better known, producers will simply call your agent and beg for you to take the role.

Meanwhile, you must make a decisive impression any way you can in circumstances that will vary enormously. Sometimes directors and agents can afford to be generous with their time and interact in your work. But often they will be harried and rushed. For you it may be the most important moment of the week, the month—even your entire career. (It isn't, of course, but it can <u>seem</u> that way.) But for the person listening, yours may be the fiftieth speech they've heard that day in a cramped and overheated room. Railing against the manifest imperfections of the audition process will not help your cause. Intelligent preparation will.

This book is a good place to start. Preparing fresh, well written material—perhaps from a play the director has heard of but hasn't even seen or read yet—is a definite advantage. It is even more important to select material that means a lot to you—something that involves a character and situation you have a strong insight into. But be careful of confusing "insight" with an intellectual or emotional sympathy with the material. Look for something that makes you say, "I know what's going on in this scene." You can flesh out the details of the story of this character from some combination of your imagination, education and experience of life.

Your audition should strive to create a carefully shaped event from a play—not just a "speech." In essence, the material should be responsive to all the things you have been trained to apply to your work in a full scale production. Because you are working alone and in a "speech" it is even more important that you ask yourself all the usual questions. What does the character want to achieve? What is the obstacle to attaining that objective and, therefore, what is the conflict of the scene? Such conflicts are usually harder to find within a monologue but you must find them. Try to find a compelling story, however simple, which will bring shape, variety and purpose to your work. If you can develop several really good pieces along these lines, you will be well on your way to making the decisive impression that can eventually lead to work.

There are some other considerations worth bearing in mind. I won't presume to speak for all directors, but I suspect my preferences are not unusual. <u>Don't</u> bring an armful of props and costumes to your audition—a single small item won't do you any harm, but your work shouldn't depend on your skill as a designer. <u>Don't</u> introduce yourself and then disappear out the door or behind a piano for a lengthy preparation. (I'm drawn to actors who can play "the moment," not those who work up emotion offstage and then regurgitate it at my feet.) <u>Don't</u> use the director as another actor in the scene without asking. I always decline this role as I find it impossible to watch objectively if I'm trying to respond to your work as a supportive actor should. <u>Do</u> try to be brisk, cheerful and efficient. <u>Do</u> try to have several additional monologues available in case a director wants to see more or different material. And above all, keep your piece short. I'd rather see several brief extracts and have a moment or two to work with you than one lengthy piece.

INTRODUCTION

And, finally, some unsolicited advice that I cannot resist, though it is bound to fall on deaf ears. By all means, work with energy and determination, but don't get suicidal if you don't get cast. Don't measure your success as a human being in terms of your success as an actor. This is an addictive, frustrating and sometimes harsh business that is worth all the sacrifices as long as it remains fun. Keep joy in your work and balance in your life. However compelling the theater may be, there are other rewards that don't revolve around the stage ... but I sense I have lost you already. So, be it. If nothing will stop you, learn to enjoy the tough road you have chosen. Work hard. See plays. Read plays. Study your craft. Work with good people whenever you can. Stay curious. And this above all, "to thine own self" ... I grow sententious. Do what you must.

The theater's a small world, I hope our paths will cross.

—David Frank
Artistic Director
American Players Theater
Spring Green, Wisconsin

THE BEST
MEN'S STAGE
MONOLOGUES
OF 1991

ADVICE FROM A CATERPILLAR
by Douglas Carter Beane
Upstate New York - Present - Suit (30's)

Suit's plans for a fun-filled weekend go awry when he finds himself playing host to Spaz, a decadent performance artist whose homosexuality makes the conservative Suit very uncomfortable. The two play Candyland while they wait for the other guests, and Suit reveals that he was somewhat less together in his youth.

SUIT: I don't really like it when she cheats. You know? She—uhm...I would like her to be above that. Not like—I don't mean to make it sound like I want her to be better than me. I mean my life is fine. Secure. I'm proud of my solidness. Not that I'm insensitive to others when they're unsolid. I mean, I've had my moments of fragility, I guess. Back in my—God, must have been sophomore year of college—Jesus, I was out there. Very erratic. Met this girl, her name was...don't even remember. Beautiful. Looked like Cheryl Tiegs. I was a mess. Just, as I said, out there. Couldn't think of anything but being with her and drinking thick red wine and making love and writing awful poems that rhymed and...what was her name? My grades were in the basement. My Dad—oh God—embarrassing memory—My Dad had to come down and give me one of those your-mother-and-I lectures. "Your mother and I" *(HE laughs)* God. I used to get those speeches semi-annually like reports. But this time my old man seemed—I don't know—pretty fragile himself. Couldn't look me in the eye. And Dad was big on eye contact. I could make eye contact before I could walk. So I broke up with the girl whose name I can't remember but who apparently was so important at the time. What can I tell you? I'm not one of those people who carry on like a French singer, right? "Life is to be lived on the edge, ho ho."

[SPAZ: Hate them.]

1

ADVICE FROM A CATERPILLAR

SUIT: *(HE stops playing, SPAZ continues)* Just doesn't appeal to me. I don't really think life needs to be so fragile. Just...keep it filled. Let's calm down and make money and let that be that. Not that I'm only a capitalist. I give back. I give back to the world.

AL PACINO
by Bryan Goluboff
New York City - Present - Leo (28)

Here, Leo tells his friend, Ricky, how Al Pacino helped to save his life.

LEO: What do I love more than anything in the world?

[RICKY: Movies...]

LEO: And who is my favorite star of all?

[RICKY: Al Pacino...]

LEO: Al Pacino...

[RICKY: So...]

LEO: He saved my life today.

[RICKY: What are you talking about? You met Al Pacino? Are you—]

LEO: Just listen to me, O.K.? You know I've been writing him the last two years, letters, ideas, sent him my journals, I wanted him to learn everything about me. I bought all this stuff at auctions. You remember that, right? *(He holds up his machine gun.)* This is the machine gun from SCARFACE. I paid $200 for it. *(He pulls out a suitcase from under the bed filled with paraphernalia. He takes out a Police Cap.)* The Police Cap he wore in SERPICO. $120. Hundreds of dollars in postage. You don't understand, Ricky... Never a reply. Nothing. When he was doing JULIUS CAESAR at the Public, I went down to see him. I wanted an answer. I couldn't get a fucking ticket. I waited outside the theatre for an hour an a half, until he came out, but I couldn't say anything. I was furious.

3

AL PACINO

I jumped in a cab and I followed him home, all the way up the west side. I saw his apartment building, everything. He got outta the cab. I was so mad, I I was gonna do something. I wanted to be recognized, you know, I wanted to alter the course of his life, but something stopped me... Today, when my mailbox was empty, I said, "Fuck this life, man." I mean, Where do you turn when your heroes let you down?

[RICKY: He's just an actor, Leo—]

LEO: Al Pacino talked to me from the screen. Why wouldn't he answer my letters? I was so sad this morning, I just wanted to end it. I wanted to get out of my own mind. I know that sounds crazy.

BABYLON GARDENS
by Timothy Mason
New York City - Present - Bill (30's)

Bill arrives home stoned and responds to his wife's concerns
about the safety of their apartment in a rambling and flippant
New York stream of consciousness.

BILL: Honest to God, taxi driver turned me on. Picked me up outside the hospital, said he works a circuit from St. Vincent's to
Bellevue to NYU Medical to Lennox Hill, he's like this stage-door
Johnny to the medical profession. Like it was his dream to be a
doctor only he drives cab instead, can you put that together? Claims
to know CPR, CVR, God knows what this guy knows, he tells me
he almost delivered two babies. He gives me a joint and I ask him
how you almost deliver a baby and he gets a little frosty. Then I tell
him I'm not a doctor and suddenly he's an iceberg. Like, why did
he offer his hard-earned weed to this asshole? So what are you, he
says, dripping contempt, an *orderly*? And I tell him I put people to
sleep and after that he doesn't say anything. Safe? What's safe?
Why should we be safe?

[JEAN: And by the time everybody gets here you won't say a word.
Which might be a blessing.]

BILL: Say you're feeling okay, *I'm* feeling okay, I get up in the
morning, maybe I'm not hungover, maybe in the night sometime you
were good to me, I woke up in the night and you were making some
kind of magic here...

[JEAN: Oh, do shut up.]

BILL: Whatever the reason, I am this morning feeling good.
Wheaties! De-caf! The sun is shining and I'm eating to win. On
the way out the door I've got my bag under one arm and the *Times*
tucked under the other and I'm whistling something from oh, the

5

BABYLON GARDENS

Gotterdammerung, probably, and bang! There's this dude on the front step with puke on his shirt asking me for change. I toss him a quarter and already there's a little dark cloud in the corner of the sky, you know what I mean? Fifteen feet later there's another one, goddammit: Gimme a quarter. Gimme your briefcase. Gimme your wife. Okay. Maybe I give him a dollar bill. Five. Wow. Show that turkey what kinda guy I really am. And suddenly I've got a headache, I've got a hangover, I'm sure I've lost my job, I'll never get it up again, and I haven't even got to the subway yet.

[JEAN: Poor you.]

BILL: Poor me? Poor them. I mean, these people out there have not found some easy scam, okay? These folks are not slogging around begging for change and sleeping in their own piss because they're feeding a secret account in some Swiss bank. They don't have *anything*. And I am, like, conflicted, you know?

THE BALCONY SCENE
by Wil Calhoun
A balcony, Chicago - Present - Alvin (30's)

An agoraphobic, Alvin has managed to live happily in the self-contained world of his apartment until vivacious Karen moves in next door. He is immediately attracted to Karen, and this eventually gives him the strength to tackle the crippling phobia that has kept him inside for years. Here, Alvin describes his first venture outside the building.

ALVIN: I'm crazy! My God, I am crazy. When I left I was fine. I felt fine. I got about halfway down the block and I lit a cigarette. There was this old woman coming the other way and she asked me for a cigarette. She called it a "cigawette". She said, "Got a cigawette?" I had one lit and the pack was in my hand. I couldn't just keep walking. So, I shook one out and it fell on the sidewalk and I didn't know if I should just give her that one, so I shook another one out and she took that one and bent down and took the other one from the sidewalk and put it in her pocket. Then she put the other one in her mouth and stood there for me to light it for her. So, I lit it, like she was my goddamn girlfriend or something and she just walked away. Didn't say thank you or anything. Just walked away. *(Alvin stops and looks at Karen for some reaction to this atrocity. She just looks at him. He continues.)* So, I got to the video store and there must have been 300 people in that place. Saturday. I forgot what Saturdays are like. I started looking around for the movies and it seemed like everywhere I went, ten people followed right behind me. It was like we were all looking for the same movies. I couldn't get away. All of a sudden, I notice this kid standing in front of me, staring at me. He's probably six or seven and he's got these glasses that have magnified his eyes about three times the normal size and he's just staring at me. He's filthy and there was stuff stuck all over his glasses. Looked like dried eggs and crumbs and God knows what else. The kid had his breakfast all over his glasses and he just kept staring at me. *(A painful reali-*

7

zation.) And I...I tried to get the hell away from him. I started to get sweaty and itchy from all the people and I had a hard time getting my breath. I had to get out. So...I bolted and I saw those people...in the street...cars and...I started walking and walking and suddenly I realized I was walking the wrong way. And...I couldn't turn around . . .

[KAREN: Alvin . . .]

ALVIN: I couldn't face...I knew I was walking the wrong fucking way and I couldn't turn around!

BLACK EAGLES
by Leslie Lee
Italy - 1941 - Roscoe (20's)

Roscoe, a member of the elite United States Air Corps Black
Eagles, is saddened by the death of a friend in a firefight. Here,
he recalls his favorite aunt for whom he also mourns.

ROSCOE: Julius, are you asleep? I need to talk.
   Remember Aunt Clara? I was really crazy about her. I liked
her better than any of my relatives. She was the only one I didn't
hide from when they came to visit. She used to pick me up when I
was a little kid, and whirl me in the air above her—around and
around and around. I felt like I was flying, and I didn't want her to
stop. "Don't stop, don't stop, Aunt Clara! Fly me all the way to
the sun please!" And she'd laugh, way down deep, and she'd say,
"Oh, no child, this old plane is coming in for a landing right now!
You'll be able to take your own self up there one day." And when
I got my license, I took her up. She didn't want to go at first. I had
to beg her. Finally, she went. And as we took off down the runway
and into the air, she started to laugh, like a young girl. "Take me
up higher and higher and higher, son. Fly me all the way to
Heaven!" And just like me, with her, she didn't want to come
down, "Because it was so peaceful, so free, so close to God." She
died not too long after that. I never had a chance to take her up
again. But sometimes, even now, when I'm up there, I can hear her
laughter, resounding all over the sky. And I know that whenever I
take off, she's up there waiting for me . . .

BLACKWATER
by J. Dakota Powell
New York City - Present - Garland Landow (40-50)

Garland, a travel writer, must watch as his life falls apart when his wife files for divorce and his publisher fires him. Here, Garland confronts his soon-to-be ex-wife.

GARLAND: Did you ever love me?
(beat)
[JEANNIE: Well of course at one point I uh—]
GARLAND: Jeannie, somehow…somewhere…things didn't change. I see a life as…a rug…not a one-color carpet, but, you know, the kinds of rugs you see old women put together stitch by stitch. I'd see them in Mombasa, perched on the rocks by the sea. It's a port town, you know, all different sorts of people mix in Mombasa— sailors, Indians, Masai warriors, bureaucrats, students, the rich, the poor, the sick—and these uh…"rugs"…were all different. Not one pattern is the same. The colors and stripes weave together in their own way…unique…and beautiful…And I used to think that if I traveled enough and saw everything the world had to offer, my life would be a rug. But now I see myself…and I look at the wrinkles that mark my face…and they don't look any different than the lines on any other old man's face…and my thoughts…they seem strung together by words I've heard before…read somewhere else…and my life…it's been lived…it's been done…so now I understand why you left…why you wanted to leave…why you had to go somewhere else every time I took a trip…because you aren't looking for comfort, Jeannie…you're still nailed to a dream. Which is why you refuse to give up on Africa. Which is why…every day…you get yourself in that godforsaken bank…and you fight and argue and compromise… for a way to make a difference. I don't do that, Jeannie. I sit back. Watch. Record. Write blurbs. Where to go. What to do. How to do it. But I never ask why. I don't need to know why. And so it takes nothing out of me. No ideas. No thought. No imagination. All I do is blame others. For what I see. For what I know. And all that takes is my time.

BLOOD ISSUE
by Harry Crews
South - Present - Pete (60's)

Joe has returned to his family home for a visit. He is looking
for clues to family ghosts which he suspects will enlighten him
about his own life. Everyone is resistant and uncomfortable.
Pete, Joe's uncle, tries to give Joe some good advice.

PETE: *(Takes a kitchen match out of his shirt pocket, chews on it,
looks at it a reflective moment, looks at JOE.)* Let me tell you a
little story you daddy—Lonny, that is to say—use to tell about
trying. *His trying-too-hard story*, he used to call it. You mighta
heard it.

[JOE: That old bastard could tell a story.]

PETE: Well, when him and Frank come back from the swamp,
Lonny got him a job with the Rural Electric Asosaytion, people that
brought lectricity to folks out in the county. Had a buddy out there
that was as close to him as somebody that ain't blood is likely to be.
Feller's name was Jake. They both had the same job, climbing and
topping trees and they was both damn good at it. Thing about Jake
though, he was bad about winning—winning at anything—bad as a
pig is about slop. Damn boy had to win. And Lonny and him got
to talking out there one day, and Lonny must've said he was faster
or some such thing and Jake said it ain't but one way to find out and
to goddammit come on. Lonny said he tried to back out two or
three times but Jake put in to try'm. You see, they'd put up poles
down the middle of the right-of-way they'd cut, but it weren't no
crosspieces on them yetawhile. Nothin'd do Jake but the two of'm
go on out there and both of'm git at the bottom of two different
poles. First one to the top was the winner. They put on their
climbing rigs, big thick safety belts that loop around the pole, inch-
and-a-half climbin jack-spikes buckled to their boots. A feller
clapped for'm and off they went. Before Jake's spikes hit the pole

11

six times, he was already two foot ahead of Lonny. See, he meant to win, so he was holding onto the safety belt that went around the pole with both hands and he was a climbing, puffing, his feet pumpin, hittin that lectric pole with them spikes driving up it, and when his feet would come up to take a fresh hold, he'd flip that leather belt with both hands and he was looking down, straight down between his pumpin knees, and never looking up and flipping that belt and driving with his feet, and when he got to the top of the pole, well, bless God, he didn't do a thing but flip that leather belt right over the top of that pole and come sailing back down on the back of his head and broke his neck. Dead fore Lonny could git down to'm. *(Pause a beat.)* That'as Lonny's *trying-too-hard* story. What do you think.

BODY AND SOUL
by John Glines
New Jersey - Present - Denny (30)

When his relationship with enigmatic Sky fails, Denny goes to
Europe where he buries himself in work and one night stands.
When he finally returns to the US, he seeks out Sky, who is
reluctant to accept Denny back into his life. During an awkward
conversation, Denny tells Sky that he made a pilgrimage to
Assisi in honor of the book Sky wrote on St. Francis.

DENNY: I went there, to Assisi, made the pilgrimage. Because of
you...He wasn't there, *Il Poverello*. Isn't that what they called him?
And *fratello*. I called one of the brothers at San Damiano *fratello*,
"brother". He corrected me, said I should call him "father", then he
sat beside me in the garden and tried to grope me...The only time I
cried was when I looked at the slab of stone in the cave where he
slept. And I had a dream that night: I dreamt of Oscar Wilde in
prison and Scott Joplin dying of penury on Welfare Island. I know
we only dream about ourselves, but still...The next day I saw three
swastikas painted on the cobblestone walls. I knew somehow that
explained it, but I didn't know how. Until I attended a lecture by
Gerta Baumann in Zurich. Oh yeah, I went to Zurich too. You
know who Gerta Baumann is, don't you? One of Carl Jung's daugh-
ters. Well, in her introduction, she said—very matter of factly—that
Nazism was the shadow of Christianity. Then it clicked. I understood: that if you recognize only the goodness of Divinity and not
the evil, there's going to be hell to pay, and in the meantime a lot of
mothers' sons are going to be imprisoned and left destitute. So I
said "Thanks, lady." I should have left then. The rest was...Well,
it was a lecture on Astrology, not one of your favorite subjects, I
know, but one of her specialties. Anyway, she had two charts on
the wall. One was her father's, the other was Oscar Wilde's. I
guess when you're gay you can't get away from Oscar Wilde. Well,
she pointed out all the wonderful things about her father as shown
in his chart, and she pointed out all the wonderful things about Oscar

13

BODY AND SOUL

Wilde in his chart, but in Oscar's chart she also found his short-comings, his flaws, I'd say his humanity. But not in her father's. He was flawless. Where was Toni Wolf in his chart, I wanted to know. You know who Toni Wolf was. Jung's mistress. Well, Frau Baumann was not about to rain on her father's parade or in anyway question her father's love for her mother, so I stood up and shouted "This is bullshit!" and walked out. But Jesus H. God, Jung wouldn't have been so dishonest, anymore than Saint Francis would have groped me in the garden of San Damiano...Please say something.

BODY AND SOUL
by John Glines
New Jersey - Present - Denny (30)

Later that same evening, Denny finally forces Sky to confront their lives and their love for one another.

DENNY: No! Now you shut up and listen!...I came here tonight to see you. I wanted to find some things changed and other things not changed a hair. And after dinner...yeah, you tried, but my defenses went up and sealed me in, and I couldn't get out. But it wasn't till Lou twisted his ankle that I knew what a total mess I'd made of it. I kept saying it was my fault. He didn't understand. But we shouldn't have been there. The whole night should have been ours, yours and mine...Look, I don't know what I want to be or do with my life—photography probably, but that's not what's important. What I do know is that I hunger to grow. I hunger to break through the limits of reasonableness, and you're the only person I've ever known who can help me do that. And this I know too, and it's something else you taught me, precious bastard: that no one can be whole without his soul, and the soul thrives only with its other side, which is always found in the Other. And when you find the Other in just one, holy mother of God, there's nothing like it! Jesus, Sky, we'd make a helluva pair. We don't need each other—I know that—but we belong together. And think how great it'd be to share things: meals, mushy movies on TV, dreams, ideas. Come on, Sky, climb down from your mountain. Climb down from that God forsaken mountain.

BREAKING UP
by Michael Cristofer
Here and Now - He (20-30)

A modern courtship—complete with all of the prerequisite trials and tribulations—culminates in the following off-handed marriage proposal.

HE: It's not going to work with her. I can see it. I mean it's working. It's working. But it's not going to work. You know?

[SHE: Jesus.]

HE: I'm going backwards.

[SHE: You want to get married to me.]

HE: I'm working at it. I'm trying. I've been trying. Honest to God. And I'm doing okay. I'm doing better than I've ever done. Better than with you. I'm patient, I'm not pushing, I'm not crazy. I'm seeing things the way they are—she is what she is, she's not who I *think* she is, she's not who I *want* her to be. We don't fight, we don't argue, we tell the truth...I think we tell the truth...We *sound* like we're telling the truth. We "share."
You know, "share." All of it. Very understanding. Like that. It's dull. Real dull.
But I'm not complaining. I'm not. If this is the way it has to be then this is what it has to be. I understand all that. I could never make anything work with the ups and downs anyway. So why not try dull? Maybe dull is the answer. Except that the truth is, you see, it's going in the same direction. It's just, when it's this dull, it's a little hard to see that it's going in *any* direction, but all this understanding, this is not going to last. A couple of words here, a couple of words there, a couple of looks, a couple of wrong moves and all of a sudden nobody understands anything anymore and you spend all your time trying to explain what you meant and what you

16

BREAKING UP

thought she meant and what you thought she thought you meant...

It has to happen. The honeymoon is over. And then you break up and you go and you find somebody else and you start all over again.

I can't do it. I did it with you. I can't do it again with somebody else. It could take years. All that time to get someplace with her that I'm already at with you. And then it hit me.

We can't quit. You and me. We have something now. We can't throw it away. It's a failure, okay, but it's ours. And it's not the end. That's too easy. It's the place to start from. It's two, two and a half years of our lives. It's an investment. All that pain to get to zero; well, now we're here, we've got nothing, nothing works, we're finished, total, complete, everything we had is gone, not a hope, not a prayer, not a chance...This is it. *(Pause)* I think we should get married.

THE CLOSER
by Willy Holtzman
New York City - Present - Howard (30-40)

Howard had purchased an apartment in a recently remodeled building in New York. Here, he arrives on moving day and recounts his harrowing experience in the cab ride from the airport.

HOWARD: Can you believe this shit? This cabbie is busting my...you're out of town three days. Not even. Two and a half days. You come back. The flight is crowded. The food I wouldn't feed to a dog. And the stewarde(ss)...excuse me, flight attendant, is, I swear, menopausal. Which is all more or less understandable given deregulation. But a cabbie? Come on. Who needs this sh(it)...needless to say, the man is not American. Not even close. No discernible nationality at all. They are a race unto themselves. Cabbies—a race apart. With bad skin, bullshit names, and attitude. Attitude all over the place. And a command of English normally associated with brain disease. What do they speak, these people? "Cabbie," is what. And this guy is busting my chops in "cabbie" because I have told him the precise fastest land route from the passenger terminal to my front step, and he is disagreeing. "No-no-no-no-no-no, me no take-ah the B-Q-E, me take-ah the..." What? He's in this country all of about seven minutes, he's telling me how to get around town. I tell him to go my way, but he doesn't comprehend because I don't speak "cabbie." And his way adds at least two bucks to the meter, which means guess what he's getting for a tip, considering the two-fifty he would've gotten? Exactly. He's looking at the tip. Suddenly his English is excellent. Suddenly we're not speaking "cabbie," we're speaking dollars and cents. "What is this?" "Two quarters. Fifty cents. Is something wrong?" "This is two quarters. My tip is two quarters—that's what's wrong." "You're right, you're right. Here." I reach over, remove a quarter. "Now your tip is one quarter. Want to go for none?" We are no longer speaking dollars and cents. We are not speaking at all. We

18

have no further basis of communication. He's in the cab. Floors it. This is a yellow cab mind you, which, if you floor it, the first thing the engine does is kind of cough at you. Picture this. The cab is coughing. The cab driver is screaming in no known language. This other cab pulls up. The driver wants to know what the problem is. I tell him the problem is the guy in the coughing cab jerked me off and it cost him two bucks in change. "You got something against cab drivers?" "I got nothing against anybody who knows how to conduct business." "I know how to conduct business." "Great—here's two and a quarter. You work it out." How does he work it out? He pockets the cash and shouts at the first cabbie: "Welcome to America—fuck you!"

THE COLORADO CATECHISM
by Vincent J. Cardinal
An artist's studio - Present - Ty (30's)

Some time after his stay at the Goodman Clinic for Alcohol and Drug Rehabilitation, Ty, an artist, tries to remember Donna, a fellow addict who helped him to change his life.

TY: A painting. A picture. A portrait. A portrait of a woman. A woman on a porch. A woman on a bone-white Victorian porch. A woman. A portrait of a woman without a woman.

I am a portrait painter. I was a portrait painter. I used to capture the quintessence of a person in a single pose, a moment. Now I only see the flaw in the elder statesman's suit, the rotting fingers under the false glossy nails of the rock star, the cowlick of this week's national child hero. I no longer see the entire person in a pose, a moment, a portrait.

I have merchandised sold and re-sold old images but this portrait of a woman is my first new work in three years. It is to prove to my backers that I am worth the investment again. To prove I can still paint. To prove I can still create. But I can't.

Artie used to say, "Man only has three absolute freedoms, darling. The freedom to love, the freedom to create, and the freedom to die by his own hand. Baby, if you ever lose painting and love, don't be so boring as to ignore suicide."

Why can't I paint? Why can't I move her from my heart, my head, my hand, to the canvas? Why should I be haunted by her for three years—three years sober and three years haunted? Why? Why? Donna, why do I always feel homesick for you?

Questions. Riddles. Secrets. Puzzles. Games.

Always back to games. Okay, okay to solve this riddle, I will play. I will play my memory like solitaire for two. Fifty-two chances. Card after Card. Memory after memory. I will search for clues, for evidence, for a moment, for a portrait of you.

The first card. The beginning. The nights were cold...The days felt like summer...But it was spring. June Second. The night

20

THE COLORADO CATECHISM

before, in Manhattan, my business associates threw a surprise party, of sorts. They had an "intervention" for me. They told me I was an alcoholic and an addict and that I had hurt them—financially. I was bankrupt. I could still paint then. But I missed deadlines, fought with clients, and destroyed a gallery full of my work at my opening party. My associates put me on a plane to Cripple Creek, Colorado and The Roger Goodman Clinic for Alcohol and Drug Rehabilitation.

Arriving in Denver, I skipped out on my enormous tab for the little bottles of whiskey I had sucked down, one after another, after another, after another. The Stewardess should have cut me off, but no one can tell when I'm drunk. I hold it well. Before the plane landed I lifted a few dozen bottles from the cart. By the time I got to Cripple Creek, I was sure the stewardess from hell was hot on my trail. In this drunken state of elevated paranoia and depressed reason—I met Donna.

THE COLORADO CATECHISM
by Vincent J. Cardinal
Rehab clinic in Colorado - Present - Ty (30's)

At the rehab center, Ty finds himself growing closer and closer
to Donna, a woman with dark secrets. When she finally asks
him to tell her about Artie, his former lover, he complies.

TY: It's just...
I keep having this nightmare...about, about those last days in New
York with Artie.
[DONNA: You said you were with Julie.]
TY: Yes. Artie's ancient history. I was just a child when we met.
Sixteen, sixteen years old. And all alone in the big scary city.
Scary, scary and sexy.
    I thought I'd live forever.
    I used to go to the clubs and get tanked up, you said that. You
said "tanked up." I used to dance like a fireball. I don't know
where it came from but something in me would happen and I'd just
blast out onto the dance floor. They'd all watch, the pretty, the
ugly, the lonely, the loved, they'd just watch me burn—a heroic
nuclear adolescent meltdown. I'd burn brilliant bright and then wake
up in somebody's bed the next morning—burnt out—with no memory
of the time between. It was a way to get by, ya know. Men,
women, black, white, old, young—I'd go with anyone.
    One grey afternoon I woke up at Artie's. He was just a little
older than I am now. I figured I'd eat and leave, maybe get a few
bucks, just like every other day, but Artie gave me my own bed,
bought me paint, even made the back of the loft a studio for me.
Artie showed me colors. Colors and light, texture, space, line,
vision. Artie gave me vision.
    Artie taught me to paint, to be an artist. He kept me in liquor,
coke, pills, anything I wanted. He got galleries to show off my stuff
and became my manager. He made me rich. Artie made me.
    I keep dreaming a new dream here, not the old one, not about
the fire. He caused it, smoking and drinking. I couldn't get him out

22

through the smoke and heat so I left him there, out cold from liquor and pills. I ran out into the street, half dressed, barefoot. I left black soot tracks in the new snow. I could see where I had been— he burned.

I used to always dream about that, or about our fights which were cruel and violent, or about sleeping in the street before Artie.

But here, I dream about the horrible, heavy sound of his breath late at night before the fire, after he "got sick." I'd hear this guttural sort of scrape in his lungs and I'd be sure he was dying there, sweating and dying there at night and I wouldn't know what to do for him. I'd lie next to him hearing him die and I'd shiver and shiver and pray to God to make him wake up and be alive. It would have killed him if it hadn't been for the fire. I think the fire was good for Artie.

But in the dream here...in the nightmare I keep having here...it isn't Artie breathing, it's me. My lungs are falling apart deep inside me. See, in the nightmare, I am sweating all the life out of me—alone in a cold bed. Anyone who ever loved me, I mean really loved me, is dead. I don't want to die like Artie.

¿DE DÓNDE?
by Mary Gallagher
Texas - Present - Teto (20's)

Teto defends his job as a Mexican-American Border Patrol agent
to Felicia, his fiancée, who has questioned his arrest of a family
trying to cross the border.

TETO: Don't you ever say that! It's what I do! It's who I am! So
face it! I've been in the Patrol for three years. What in the name
of Christ did you think I did out there? *(They stare at each other;
finally.)* You want out of this?
[FELICIA: I don't know.]
[TETO: Jesus.]
[FELICIA: Do you?]
TETO: You can't put me through this. You've gotta accept it, and
that's the end of it.
[FELICIA: Why? Why is that the only way—?]
TETO: Because I love this job! It *made* me! All the work I ever
had was dumb-ass, shit-paid crap, I was bored out of my mind, you
know that, Christ, I was a maniac!—drinking like a fucking loon—
sometimes your parents wouldn't even let me see you!
[FELICIA: But that's because you're better than those stupid jobs,
if you'd just—]
TETO: *(Overlap.)* I am a chicano! I'm in Texas! I barely made
it out of high school! Half my friends are out of work! Sometimes
I dream I'm picking fucking grapefruit—would that make you happy?
[FELICIA: You could go to college—]
TETO: *(Grabs her.)* [No!] See me for who I am! Felicia, the
Patrol...it's like I'm finally home. It's respect! It's honor. Anglos
look up to me—my father never had that!...and security, for you and
me, for our kids—'cause once you're in, the brothers are always
gonna stick by you, no matter what! And it's even more than that
...I feel like it's my calling. When I'm on night patrol, out there in
the fields along the river, and the sky is all over me, and I can't hear
a sound...but every part of me is listening...and watching for the

24

¿DE DÓNDE?

signs...I'm so alive, so happy! and powerful and free—for the first time since I was a kid, I'm free! And it's an adventure! Every time, it's new—you don't know what you're gonna find—
[FELICIA: But what you find is people.]
TETO: *(Beat; then.)* I don't have to justify myself to you. *(Pause.)*
[FELICIA: Well ... goodnight, I guess—]
TETO: Terrific! Hey, thanks for stopping by! Maybe I'll get the hatchet and hack the fucking walls in!
[FELICIA: *(Close to tears.)*...Well, I don't know what else to say ...]
TETO: Could you just *shut up?* Just *be* here? *(Pause. She moves to him, they embrace. Beat; then.)* You are such a *woman,* Felicia! You've got everything in you, if you'd just quit fighting it!
[FELICIA: Fighting *what?*]
TETO: Me! The family...the Valley...You grew up on the river just like I did, in the middle of the same big, crazy family, and there's just no way to get that out of you! But you're so fierce, so goddamn smart and ornery...you just can't give in to us and let us make you happy.
[FELICIA. It's not that simple ...]
TETO: *(Continues.)* I love you so goddamn much! I love it that you're a fighter—just quit fighting me.

THE GEOGRAPHY OF LUCK
by Marlane Meyer
Las Vegas - Present - Dixie (30's)

When Dixie returns to his home in Las Vegas after having
served a prison term for strangling his wife, he discovers that
his mother, once a beautiful Vegas showgirl, has died. Dixie
struggles to come to terms with his past and his feelings for his
parents.

DIXIE: I thought I saw my mother in a bar the other day but she
ignored me when I tried to say hello. She was sitting with a man,
and I was watching them and they were silent with each other, you
know the way couples are. And I watched that man till I could see
through his eyes, my father's eyes, and this woman, she made a joke
to him, and he turned away. Cold. And I could feel myself
becoming afraid, I could feel his fear. Of her intimacy. 'Cause I
was not worthy, *he* was not worthy.

And I could feel him become angry with her and it moved me.
I went up to him, and asked him, where did he learn to be
worthless? Where did he learn to be unworthy of love?

And he stood up, and he stared at me, at my arms and my fists
and he turned to the woman, and he jerked her up and accused her
of flirting with me by making herself congenial to him. And then he
slapped her. Hard. And I felt that slap sting my cheek, and my
father's cheek, and my father's father's cheek, all the way down the
line, I saw dead men reel under the weight of that blow, 'cause
jealousy, Dutchy, is a curse.

GROTESQUE LOVESONGS
by Don Nigro
Terre Haute, IN - 1980's - Pete (27)

Pete has just learned that his younger brother, John, is not his
father's son. Romy, John's fiancée, whom Pete secretly desires,
offers some unsolicited advice. Pete snaps back.

PETE: I hate it when people who are not where I am, who have
never been where I am and who will never be where I am try and
tell me it isn't really as bad where I am as I think it is. You are not
where I am, so don't talk to me about it, and you were certainly not
on my honeymoon, and I don't want to hear a bunch of stupid shit
from somebody who wasn't there about what it was or wasn't like
or how I should feel about it. In fact, I don't want to hear anything
you've got to say, so why don't you just get the hell out of here and
leave me alone?

GROTESQUE LOVESONGS
by Don Nigro
Terre Haute, IN - Summer 1980 - Pete (27)

When Pete returns home alone after leaving to marry a woman
he met at a carnival, his family can only wonder what went
wrong and why she left him. After many months of silence,
Pete confesses the truth to Romy, his brother's fiancée and the
woman he has always loved.

PETE: You and Johnny were watching television in the dark and I
didn't want to hang around so I took a walk down towards the
carnival and in the grass by the parked cars I found a girl, she had
a black eye and she was bleeding and crying. She lived with this
carny guy who had Japanese dogs tattooed all over him and he'd get
drunk and beat her up. We got to talking and one thing kind of led
to another. I brought her home once but Mom couldn't stand her.
She was scared the carny guy was gonna come after her so I took
some money out of the bank and we got in my van and drove west.
The trip was great, we stopped to see whatever she liked, she had a
great capacity for enjoying things, I loved to watch her, she—
enjoyed them completely while they were happening. We spent
some time in Arizona and then she wanted to drive up to Las Vegas
and get married, so we did, in this little chapel, and she wanted to
see a show, so we went, a lot of naked women with too much on,
loud music, I didn't like it, but mostly I was watching her, her face
was kind of bathed in this red light, from the show, we were sitting
real close, in the red light, and she was like a beautiful animal. At
intermission they had a contest for couples in the audience, they'd
get in these big potato sacks together, tied up under their arms, and
some guy would shoot off a gun and they'd have to hop across the
stage towards these enormous piles of silver dollars, and they could
stuff as many in their sack as they wanted, but they had to hop back
across to where they started, and the couple who got there first got
to keep all the silver dollars in their sack. I never saw such carnage
in my life. One guy fell over and spilled some on the stage and his

28

GROTESQUE LOVESONGS

wife was beating him with both fists and screaming at him, frothing at the mouth, horrible, and I looked over at my wife and she was laughing and clapping her hands together like a child, and her eyes were gleaming like a cat's. She'd had a lot to drink and she smelled like perfume and alcohol and sex and she turned her head in the red light and looked at me. We went up to our room and made love all night, she was absolutely wild for it, scratching and biting and screaming, I was bleeding all over the sheets. When I woke up in the morning she was gone, her clothes were gone, the money was gone, my car was gone. I was stupid, I thought the carny guy had found us, so I went to the police station and showed them a picture of her, and they were very gentle, they said, Son, you ain't married, this girl's got more husbands than you got fingers and toes. She works with this guy with tattoos, brings em here, takes their money and dumps em. I walked out onto the highway and started hitch-hiking east, and when I got home I went into the greenhouse and started to work, and I've been here ever since, in my father's garden. This is a green world, I can deal with this, but no more animals, nothing that bleeds, not ever.

KINGFISH
by Marlane Meyer
Wylie's home - Present - Wylie (50's)

When Wylie returns home after being mugged, he is greeted by his faithful Kingfish: a rather large Doberman. Here, Wylie tells his story to Kingfish, who barks constantly.

WYLIE: NOBODY LIKES TO BE BY HIMSELF!
(barking stops)
But sometimes it's necessary. You understand that, don't you?! I got MUGGED.   Robbed in the dark.   Scrawny arms covering balding pate, knocked out and sealed like some kind of sardine in the trunk of my car, dirty, tired, drenched in piss I come home and what do I find?!
MY GODDAMN SLIPPERS AND MY GODDAMN NEWS-PAPER!
(he drops the slippers and paper and makes a drink)
If you want an outlet...chew your tail. I am sick and tired of being a loser.
(silence)
(he drinks as he watches the dog)
WYLIE: Oh don't pout, I hate that.
(bark)
(snorts)   The police...!   I told them I'd been robbed of my Hasselblad, they said, what's that? I said it's a camera you mafia kingpin, where's Jimmy Hoffa, oh it was really funny to them...
(bark bark)
Drinking, drinking but not drunk.
(Bark bark bark)
Yes, I'm sure he stole it. What do you think it slipped up my asshole when I wasn't looking?
(Wiley touches his head)
See this?
Emergency hospital.   Three hundred and fifty-nine dollars.   And they don't want to touch me.

30

KINGFISH

This quack is a mass of keloids and he doesn't want to touch ME?
Christ!
(he grimaces)
"Picking up hitchhikers for purposes of an immoral nature can be
very dangerous, Mr. Wylie."
Prissy cunt, safe sex, fuck me harder.
(bark bark)
WYLIE: *(defensive)* Driving. Just driving around, that's all.
(bark bark)
Oh, it's nothing like you imagine it's all become so ordinary. It's
so much about just a little chat these days. Just a little talk. Lonely
for the sound of a human voice, needing more than a drive through
the park on a dark night, like some kind of night crawler, hideous,
glow in the dark, fishing, fishing but never catching.
(bark bark)
Companionship, is that too much to ask?
(bark, bark, bark)
(kindly) You're a dog, like a fish, animal kingdom, woof woof, you
have your limitations, I mean dogs don't dream, I have dreams...
(bark)
Oh, you think EVERYTHING is bullshit. *(pointedly)* I am an old
man now. I wasn't this morning. Comprende?
(Wylie lights a cigarette, coughs viciously)
So.
As I am unsafe about my person, you shall be trained in the ways of
the Ninja beast.
(whine)
Oh stop that...
(bark bark)
WYLIE: You're not THAT old.
(bark bark bark)
No I will not remain indoors for the duration. The duration of
what...? Oh my God. *(beat)*
(He cries and whines under Wylie's speech)

31

KINGFISH

The world is a whore riding to hell on the back of a cockroach. Each day hundreds die at the hands of total strangers. Food chains rule with impunity, big fish to little fish, killing the weak, eating the old, but where preparation meets opportunity, there lies the intruder, his throat in shreds, awash in a sea of his own bodily fluids.
(the barking ceases, Wylie moves downstage, stares out)
You'd like to see these young sonsabitches face down on the concrete, the black boot at the base of THEIR skull, looking out of the inky pit for mercy and finding none, imploring ME, begging ME, they think they can fuck with ME, they can't fuck with ME.
(Bark bark bark bark)
(beat, coldly, he turns) You sound...like an old man's dog.

LA BÊTE
by David Hirson
Languedoc, France - 1654 - Elomire (30-50)

When Prince Conti decrees that his theatrical troupe be joined by
Valere, a vulgar troubadour, Elomire is so offended that he tells
the Prince that he must decide between the mediocrity of Valere
and the excellence of his own work. Unfortunately, Elomire
soon discovers that everyone in his troupe is more interested in
preserving their cushy lives at court than in his own integrity.
Here, the defeated Elomire prepares to leave the estate to face
life as a wandering player.

ELOMIRE *(This final speech is spoken quietly, to himself)*:
By starting on a journey once again
(Not knowing what's to come, or where I'm bound)
I wonder—did I stand too firmly, then,
When this safe haven had at last been found?

Does any way less radical exist
To keep ideals from being trivialized?
The only way I know is to *resist*:
Autonomy cannot be compromised!

*(Elomire lifts his head to see Dorine, who has never left the stage
and is standing in the shadows, listening.)*
ELOMIRE:
With every day the peril is increased
Of yielding to this treacherous misrule,
For fools contain inside of them a beast
That triumphs when the world is made a fool!

(A low murmur of voices and laughter is heard from the other room.)
ELOMIRE:
If LIFE—not grim survival—is the aim,
The only hope is setting out to find

33

LA BÊTE

A form of moral discourse to reclaim
The moral discourse fools have undermined.

Upon that road I joyfully embark!
And though it seems that joy itself's at stake,
There's joy itself in challenging the dark:
We're measured by the *choices* that we make!

(An eruption of laughter from offstage. Dorine slowly crosses to Elomire, carrying his belongings to him.)
ELOMIRE:
Against great odds one gamely perseveres,
For nature gives advantage to a fool:
His mindless laughter ringing in your ears,
His thoughtless cruelties seeming doubly cruel;

His power stems from emptiness and scorn—
Debasing the ideals of common men;
But those debased ideals *can* be reborn . . .
By starting on the journey once again.

THE LAST GOOD MOMENT OF LILY BAKER
by Russell Davis
A country inn - 1980 - Sam (36)

Sam and Molly have a reunion with their friends, Bob and Lily, at the same country inn where both couples spent their honeymoons. When Sam notices that Lily seems depressed, he lectures Bob on the pitfalls of a sad wife.

SAM: No, things happen, Bob. Lots of things happen. They can leap out of nowhere. We don't even want to admit them, talk about them, nothing, because they can take you out of the picture. And the picture is business. We're meant to do business. It's fun. Every time I take a plane I look out the porthole and there's business. The fields, the desert, they're divided for business. Nothing is any longer just trees and bugs and animals. And there has to be a reason for that. Which is we need to take our minds off the things we can do absolutely nothing about. Like if a car hits into us, or one of our children. Or if a wife goes sad on us. Business is what protects us. Because business is the only thing we have left to keep our attention going and focused on something we can do something about.
(Pause.)
SAM: Lily's taking you out of the picture, Bob. From the very beginning she took you out. There was no reason you had to go to a state college. You could have gone away. You could have gone to the world.
(Pause.)
SAM: Bob, on the way here yesterday we got lost. Molly and I, in the car. And we argued. Our memories clashed on which way we drove fifteen years ago. And finally I pulled into this farmhouse. Nice white farmhouse where there was no more farming. Just two guys living. Young big fellows. Big plaid shirts. Healthy. Seemed like no wives. And they came out to ask what we wanted. These two guys. So they gave us directions, and we drove ahead. But, Bob, it reminded me a hell of a lot, in the deepest way, of what we used to have. When there were directions, simple directions, any-

35

where you wanted to go, and there were still all these choices. Simple choices. Sometimes I think the promise I had, the expectation, got interrupted when I married Molly.

THE LAST GOOD MOMENT OF LILY BAKER
by Russell Davis
A country inn - 1980 - Sam (36)

Here, Sam reveals to Bob that he has always desired Lily, Bob's
wife.

SAM: Bob, listen. I remember when we painted your parents'
house. We were up on ladders painting their house. And Lily was
down below. She was watching us. She was keeping us company,
and I think it was about the first time you and she were together. I
could tell you were together. And I know it was funny. It was
funny to joke later about how I fell off the ladder. 'Cause we took
it like a couple of guys. Cracked Humpty Dumpty jokes. Took a
picture even. Reenacted it, the next day. But actually I think my
thoughts were pretty complicated up there. Serious. And I had a
concussion. I don't think we realized that, a concussion, lying there
on the ground. And it's like that thing when you think you might
die. Or you're caught between two worlds. 'Cause I don't remember the ground, or the lawn, any of that. I remember, clearly,
that I stood in the middle of a field. I was standing distinctly in a
field. In the middle of nowhere. And I had in my hand a doorknob.
That's all I had. A doorknob, for some reason. No door, no house,
just the doorknob. And then Lily came up to me. In this field.
And she said she noticed something. She wanted to tell me. So I
asked her what she noticed. And she said out there, Sam, is a last
good moment. And I said, what? And she said, out there, at the end
of the field. And she said it again, like I was dumb or something.
So I looked out toward the end of the field, to see if I could see this
moment, whatever moment she meant. And I saw there were trees,
and some pond off to the side. And then I thought I noticed it too.
I thought I noticed what Lily noticed. And when I realized that, the
trees at the end of the field got suddenly closer. I was standing right
underneath them. And then these things fell off me. Like my
memory. Like my understanding of why an airplane should work,
or a car. Taxes. Doors. The doorknob. People behaving on the

37

earth. Those kinds of understandings just fell off me. Like a dirty T-shirt. Some kind of T-shirt. And underneath was my chest. This feeling in my chest. And I thought, Christ, I think I'm going to see something. I'm going to see sights. I'm going to see all kinds of shapes and sizes, things that hang out and heave out there. Things behind what I think I see out there. I'm going to see influences.
(Pause.)
SAM: When I woke up on the ground at the foot of your house, Bob, I saw Lily. She was leaning over me, concerned. And behind her head was the sky. She was with me beneath the sky. And I remember her eyes. Like high school. Eager like high school. Like it was the end, the end of all conception, or thinking, and at the end is this eagerness. Waiting for me. This simplicity.
(Pause.)
SAM: I think that hurt me. That simplicity.
(Pause.)
SAM: I think sometimes about the Inquisitor. The Grand Inquisitor. The guy who had to tell Christ that simplicity could hurt people.
(Pause.)
(SAM closes the balcony door.)
SAM: Personally, Bob. I'll tell you what I notice. What I see. I see a Doberman. I keep seeing this Doberman follow me.

LIFE DURING WARTIME
by Keith Reddin
An apartment - Present - Howard (16)

Howard and his mother, Gale, decide to look into a home security system. As the salesman describes the system to Gale,
Howard returns home and preceeds to tell them a wild tale of
being abducted.

HOWARD: Yeah. Hey, Mom, guess what happened today.
[GALE: What?]
HOWARD: Come on, guess.
[GALE: Tell me.]
HOWARD: [Okay.] Barry and me after school, we're driving
around. We're driving on the Parkway and we're in the left lane
and Barry's going fast, maybe a little too fast I say Barry slow
down, but he's trying to pass this car in the passing lane and it
doesn't move over, so Barry puts on his lights, he's flashing his
lights at this guy to pull over so we can pass and I go Barry, take it
easy, but now like Barry is pissed, and we are tooling along and this
other car it pulls alongside us and there's some guys in there and
they are very pissed off so we take off dueling back and forth like
who can get in front of the other and Barry he goes mental and tries
to push this car onto the shoulder and then he sort of bumps the car,
well he crashes into the side of it, and we both pull over and Barry
is incensed but I tell Barry I want to just get the fuck out of here and
we get out and the guys from the other car get out only there's four
of them and two of us, and this one guy the driver goes up to Barry
and puts his face close to Barry's face and says you fucked with the
wrong person today and these guys push Barry and me up against
their car and then from out of their trunk they take this wire and
they tie our hands behind our backs and they hit Barry in the head
and they put us in the trunk and say we're going for a ride fuckface
and they drive us for about half and hour and then I hear this gravel
crunching and we stopped and they open the trunk and these four
guys push us out into these woods and Barry's pissing in his pants

LIFE DURING WARTIME

and I'm thinking we're dead you know, so this guy with funny teeth
he pulls out a gun and he puts it to Barry's head and tells him hey
pussy you scraped the side of our car what are you going to do about
it and Barry and me we don't say nothing and these other guys say
if we don't want to die we have to eat dirt and so we do, we eat dirt
and these other guys get real quiet and watch us eat dirt and then
they piss on Barry and they push this gun in Barry's face and then
they smoke some cigarettes and don't talk then they get in their car
and drive off. And after a while we get up and start walking down
the road and look for a cop car but we couldn't find one so we start
hitching and we get a ride and we walk a ways to Barry's car with
this huge damage done to its side and he drives back to here and tells
me not to say anything about this ever, but it's just too incredible
you know, so I'll be in my room till dinner.

LOVE LEMMINGS
"What He Wants"
by Joe DiPietro
Here and Now - Man (30's)

When a woman seeking a simple sexual encounter approaches a strange man in a bar, she is totally unprepared for the tirade with which he meets her simple proposal.

MAN: *(After a moment)* What I want? You want to know what I want?

[WOMAN: That's right, sweet meat.]

MAN: Okay. Okay, fine. You know what I want? I want to know what exactly the rules are nowadays?

[WOMAN: Pardon?]

MAN: I mean when I was growing up in the '50's, it was Father Knows Best time and the rules were simple: the man paid for everything and you didn't get laid until you were married so everyone got married at like 16 and fine, I could deal with women as housewives.

[WOMAN: Wait, you didn't understand the question.]

MAN: But then came the '60's and we all did a lot of drugs and made a lotta love and I'd look out my window and there'd be this mountain of bras on fire! So okay fine, I could deal with women as liberated.

[WOMAN: Oh, no—]

MAN: Then it was the '70's and the E.R.A. and Alan Alda and you all wanted your own careers so you could be just as miserable as

41

LOVE LEMMINGS

men! Okay, fine, I could deal with women as equals!

And then the '80's and Ronald Reagan rules the roost for eight LOOOONG YEARS, and all of a sudden, WHAMO, we're back in the Father Knows Best '50's again, except this time carrying a lot of baggage from the '60's and '70's! And now we're SMACK in the '90's and I'm nothing but totally confused!! I mean, am I supposed to be sensitive or macho or what? Do I pull out the chair, do I open the car door, do I ask if you've orgasmed?!

When a woman offers to split the check, does she really mean it, OR IS SHE JUST TESTING ME?!

AND HOW COME NO MATTER HOW LIBERATED THE WOMAN IS, I'M STILL ALWAYS THE ONE WHO HAS TO KILL THE BIG BUGS IN THE BATHROOM!

SO YOU KNOW WHAT I WANT?! I JUST WANT TO KNOW WHAT THE HELL IT IS YOU ALL WANT?!

LOVE LEMMINGS
"First A Clock, Then..."
by Joe DiPietro
Here and Now - Doug (30's)

Doug and Jackie go shopping together and find a clock that
Jackie falls in love with. Doug offers to buy it for her, but after
a moment's reflection, begins to fear that this simple purchase
may lead to further commitments.

DOUG: Wait stop! Jackie, you're—you're right! Wait, stop! I
mean, before it was all just dinners and dating and sleeping together.
Ya know, the usual. But now, oh God now, Jackie— we're on the
verge of making a joint purchase—we're about to become: a
couple—

[JACKIE: Yeah—]

(JACKIE goes to kiss him again; he stops her.)

DOUG: You with the credit cards, stop right there! — Jackie, let's
talk about this first, okay. I mean, sure, now it's just a clock, but
next maybe we'll get a VCR, and so you start spending lots of time
at my place watching old musicals and all of a sudden I look in my
closet and it is filled with your shoes. Then we get bored of the
VCR but we see the cutest fish in this aquarium so we get that and
now you're spending all your time at my place staring at our cute
fish and no sooner than I look in my medicine cabinet but it is
stocked with your tampons.

[JACKIE: Well, is that all so terrible?]

DOUG: [Well, no, no, but] then we say, what the hell! We got the
clock and the VCR and the aquarium, we might as well get married.
And before we even have time to figure out what we want, we're
standing in front of cousins we don't even know vowing that we're

43

LOVE LEMMINGS

forever!

[JACKIE: Doug—]

DOUG: Then we move the clock and the VCR and the aquarium into our new co-op your parents helped pay for and we swear we'll never leave the city because the suburbs mean death, but then we'll have children—like four of 'em!—and we'll realize the city is no place to raise four kids so we'll decide the suburbs aren't so lethal after all so we'll move to Long Island and get this huge mortgage and you'll bail out of your career cause you have to stay home with our four kids cause if you don't they won't score well on their S.A.T.'s and they'll have to go to their safety schools! And I'll grow gray and fat and bitter and we'll never again have spontaneous sex and I'll start voting Republican and I'll spend my weekends mowing and spackling and grouting and caulking and driving our four kids and their twenty friends to the mall and we won't ever again have oral sex and I'll start watching bowling on t.v. and soon our four kids will resent me for not spending enough time with them so they'll start listening to heavy metal music for the satanic messages and we won't ever again have sex of any kind and I'll never play for the Yankees and I'll fall ln love with this 22-year-old graduate student who I met in the video store but she won't have anything to do with me unless I get a divorce, but by then I won't be able to cause I'll feel far too trapped in our loveless, sexless suburban marriage with our four satan-worshipping kids! And that's it—end of life, end of story! You might as well just bury me now!

LUCY LOVES ME
by Migdalia Cruz
Bronx - Present - Milton (20's)

Here, Milton reveals his tendency towards sexual deviation as he relaxes in his tub.

MILTON: What will I do tonight? Hello. Hello. I'm only doing this for you. I don't always do this. It's my favorite day. My day of all days. It's Goosey Night. Mischief night. Guess what I'm wearing. Yes? Yes? Yes, of course. Of course, the white gold. Not the gold gold. Who would wear that? Who'd be caught dead in such a get-up? I got back early from the store. To have enough time. To have the time to get everything. I stay younger with the blood from a cock in my bath. But it takes time. So much ritual. Everyone names everything. There is a formula. You take out the gizzards after it's sliced through the neck. But the gizzards are at the other end. Why not go in that way? Why not go in through the back door and cut up? Rules. There are rules for everything. Jack the Ripper broke the rules—had consented sex before he killed his women. Better to rape I think. First. Give them a little psychological preparation as it were. A bit of warning. I always wanted to rape a woman, but I never could. I wanted to have that God-like power. Did God love Mary? I wonder. He invaded her. I'm sure of that.

45

LUSTING AFTER PIPINO'S WIFE
by Sam Henry Kass
A big city - 1989 - Vinnie (30)

Here, Vinnie encounters Patsy and Rita on the street, and having been referred to by Patsy as "an interesting guy," proceeds to regale them with his unique insight into the complexities of modern relationships.

VINNIE: Did he tell you that, Rita? He honestly told you that, huh?

[RITA: Yes...]

VINNIE: Isn't he a sweetheart? What a nice thing to say. *(Pause)* You don't usually hear guys talk that way 'bout one another. Especially, there's a lovely young lady involved.

[RITA: What do you mean?]

[PATSY: He just ...]

VINNIE: *(Cutting him off)* You see, men are cut from a different loin of cloth...They don't usually create a scenario that many times throughout history, has come back to haunt them. A man is with a woman, as Patsy seems to be with you...He meets his best friend on the street, introduces him to the mystery woman. The woman already has a semblance of knowledge, concerning the aforementioned best friend: that he's "a real interesting guy." So already the groundwork is laid...Perhaps there's some sort of initial chemistry between the friend and the mystery woman. Perhaps it's so buried, so hidden that neither one even recognizes its presence. Perhaps these two newly introduced creatures of our societal jungle—will bid each other farewell, after only minutes of introductory chit-chat, only to go through the remainder of that day, and the following day, and then who knows how many days after, only to be burdened with

LUSTING AFTER PIPINO'S WIFE

the sexual magnetism that makes two people prisoners of passion... *(Pause)* More than likely, that fire eventually burns out. And all that remains are ashes, of what might have been...However, there are those occasions, as history has documented—where these two benighted and tortured souls have no choice but to seek each other out—find one another, track each other to the earth's end, because there is no other choice. The human being is a very complicated situation. Should never be glossed over, with a wave of the hand. The powers they must wrestle with are stronger than each of us individually... *(Pause)* Just some food for thought.

LUSTING AFTER PIPINO'S WIFE
by Sam Henry Kass
A big city - 1989 - Vinnie (30)

Pipino is an illegal alien who washes dishes in Vinnie's bistro. Vinnie enjoys carrying on long, one-sided conversations with Pipino, who doesn't speak English. Here, Vinnie reveals his fascination with Pipino's wife.

VINNIE: *(Calling out)* Hey, Pipino...What's the good word? What's happening? Bueno. Yeah, yeah...Mucho bueno. How's that wife of yours?—You keeping her happy? *(Gives him a hand signal)* You still give it to her every night? No kidding...You married her young, right? She's never been with any other man? Just you, all these years? You think that's fair, Padre? I know she's your wife—But you married her at what...She was eleven years old? Go 'head, start on those dishes. Yeah, go 'head...You see, you can't do that to a woman. They resent you, for the rest of their life. You can't take a woman that young, never let her be with no one else. It's not healthy. Emotionally...You know what I'm saying? Don't play stupid, alright? I mean, let's have a conversation. I'm trying to treat you like an equal. Pipino, listen to me...I'm trying to save your marriage. You want your wife to be happy, no? So this is what you got to do—Before it's too late, you gotta give her some freedom. Like a bird. Never mind the pigeons. I'm talking about your wife. You gotta let her be with someone else. Just to get it out of her system...Another man. For your wife...It's good for her. She'll love you more. Makes the marriage stronger. Stronger marriage. Right...You told me she's always asleep, anyways. Right? Your wife—She sleeps when you...When you fuck your wife—She sleeps right through it, no? Yeah, that's what you told me. Then you see what I'm talking about, right? Pipino? You see what I'm saying? Everybody needs a change, now and then...Yeah, right. Don't thank me. It's okay. Listen...Your wife ever mention me?—She talk about Señor Vinnie? Yeah, Mr. Vinnie. She likes me, no? Of course she likes me. Yeah, that's what I thought.

LUSTING AFTER PIPINO'S WIFE

Maybe you'll have me over to the house, one day. To your house.
Yeah, casa...Right. We're all family, here...Familio...All of us
we're family. Yeah, yeah...Alright, go finish the dishes.

MARRIAGE LINES
by Donald Churchill
London - Present - Tony (42)

Tony, awaiting a rare visit from a very successful friend and his wife, responds to a comment from his sympathetic wife that the pain in his hand is probably his rheumatism acting up. He reveals the recent onslaught of mid-life crisis.

TONY: It's not my rheumatism that is making my hand ache, it's because I've gone onto a more difficult lesson. Because it's unfamiliar, not because I'm cracking up. *(Stares defiant, haunted, turns back to her.)* I'm sure it's lack of practise. My rheumatism has only ever been in my right shoulder . . . never in my hand. My fingers shouldn't start getting stiff yet should they? At 42!

[RUTH: *(Reading.)* Lack of practise, darling...added to that it's been a damp day. Nothing to worry about.]

TONY: I've never, never had a twinge of anything in my right hand...till I started the guitar. I've jogged our bed up and down for 20 years...never had a twinge of anything—except in my shoulder. I shall have a Dubonnet. *(He pours out the drink.)* I haven't got rheumatism in my hand. God! I had to pack up the clarinet because it made me breathless, now I've got to pack up the guitar because of rheumatism! Ridiculous! I'm in the prime of my life! The peak of my halcyon days! *(Sips his drink...stares ahead.)* I was puffed this morning though running up the office stairs!

[RUTH: Never mind, darling...you've still got me.]

[TONY: With your lumbago.]

[RUTH: *(Puts magazine down.)* Oh darling...don't!]

TONY: *(Sulking.)* Well stop going on about my rheumatism then.

MARRIAGE LINES

(Pause.) A thought occurred to me today at work. A genuine thought...if I sold my business, after paying all debts, I'd walk away with an overdraft of £2000. 15 years running my own business and if I sold up tomorrow...I'd still owe money. The thought made me so depressed, I had to go out and have a dover sole and a bottle of Chablis on my Barclaycard.

[RUTH: I had a boiled egg for lunch.]

TONY: *(Reflective.)* Dover sole and broccoli spears. *(Pause. Smacks his lips. Slight pause.)* When I started my business, I was convinced I'd make a fortune. Don't know where I've gone wrong. *(Pause.)* I've got a smashing personality! People love telling me their problems...so many people...over the years, have said to me... Tony...I really do feel so much better now, having talked to you!

[RUTH: They do, darling. You're lovely in times of trouble. *(Turns a page.)* T't. How ridiculous!]

TONY: I am! *That is true!* So why haven't I made any money?

[RUTH: Why do you suddenly want money?]

TONY: I've always wanted money. Particularly now my rheumatism is spreading. Any day now I shall start smelling of old age...like Aunty Edith...the sweet smell of corsets.

[RUTH: We have enough money, darling...more than most.]

TONY: *(Stares out.)* I sat in the Dolce Vita restaurant today all on my own in the corner...just me and my copy of the Exchange and Mart...and I thought about when I was 25. I was so sure... then, that by the time I was 40 I'd be able to retire and lead the life of a scholar and a gentleman. How *could* I have been so convinced?

51

MARRIAGE LINES

That's what troubles me!

[RUTH: Was this half way through your sole?]

TONY: Half way through my brandy. I ended up absolutely astonished. I still am astonished. Astonished that *I* have been such a disappointment to myself. *(Shakes his head in wonder.)*

MARRIAGE LINES
by Donald Churchill
London - Present - Bill (40ish)

Anne, a house guest of Tony and Ruth, has just been discovered
by Ruth in a funny kind of sleep. Bill, a dentist friend, has just
arrived for a golfing date with Tony. Bill realizes that Anne has
attempted suicide and calls the hospital.

BILL: Casualty department please. Good morning...A friend of
mine is bringing in a woman who appears to have taken an overdose
of sleeping tablets. Should be with you in about five minutes.
(RUTH enters with a handbag and a pill bottle.) Yes. Pretty sure.
I'm a dentist by profession and I suspect some type of barbiturate
poisoning. *(Takes bottle.)* The bottle is empty... but it's the 50
capsule size...no, I don't know what sort. *(With one hand he tips up
Anne's handbag onto sideboard.)* No! Hold on!...green...yes I've
found what looks like empty capsules of Tuinal...Taken 15 minutes
ago and in powder form...yes...the effect was so quick. Yes...it
does look as if she means to do it! Obviously emptied every capsule
into a glass and taken the lot with water...for quicker absorption.
My name? Davenport... William Davenport...but I'm only ringing
up as a private individual asking you stand by to pump her out.
There's no reaction from her Achilles tendon...and from what I
gather, she was in a highly neurotic and hysterical state so she's
likely to metabolize the drug very quickly...Well, I think unless
she's pumped out within the next half hour she's a goner. My
number? It's 398 1178...but no—you see I'm not there...I'm at 398
3294... Very nice of you...No...don't ring 398 1178 my wife will...
it'll only confuse her...yes...here at 398 3294...thank you...*(Hangs
up.)* They're going to ring me here. Do hope they do. That Indian
doctor wanted to ring me at home...as if I'm not in enough trouble.
My God! If they ring Maggie and tell her that some lady friend of
mine has...she'd go for me with her scissors...the mood she's in
now...she'd shove her pinking shears right in me. *(Sorts through
contents of Anne's handbag.)* Neat girl. She's put all the empty
capsules in an envelope. Let's count her capsules. Got a cup of
coffee in that pot?

53

NEBRASKA
by Keith Reddin
SAC base, Omaha, NE - Present - Swift (30's)

Swift has known the military all his life and has limited understanding of events occurring outside his daily Air Force routine. Here, he tells the sad tale of having to kill his dog.

SWIFT: I had to kill my dog today. Gidget was close to seventeen, my wife says it was more like eighteen, that's old for a dog. My folks had taken her for the time we were in Germany, and then we brought her out here. And day by day, you could see she was getting worse. First she got kind of blind, walking into the middle of the street, car horns blasting, trucks whizzing a couple of inches from her, walking into closed doors, knowing the door was there, not seeing it was closed. Then the back legs gave out. She started dragging her body around, limping and huffing, falling down. Finally she could hardly get up. I had to pick her up just to get her outside, into the sun, Gidget sitting on this old blanket not lifting her head, making these sounds, you know, groans and sighs, cause she knew she was going. So today, I lifted her up, put her in the back of the car, drove out Route 24 to this field, lay her down, shot her right behind the ear. I didn't think about it. I just shot her. Smoked a cigarette and waited till I knew her soul had left her. Rolled her up in the blanket, put her in the trunk, drove home. Buried her. Had dinner. We talked about another dog, but I told Julie to wait a while. I'd had Gidget so long. So she's out back now, under the dirt.

OUR OWN KIND
by Roy MacGregor
England - Present - Ollie (40-50)

A kind-hearted bus driver, Ollie seems to have won his battle against loneliness. Here, he prepares for an evening of roller-skating.

(Kitchen, later. Lorna is at the table, studying. Ollie enters, dressed up ready to go out. He gives his shoes a final brush.)
OLLIE: Friday night—magic. A man needs an interest, Lorna. Something more than just an evening slumped in front of the box. When you think of the state I was in after your Mum did a runner ...I was gutted. Should have seen it coming, of course. I'm too trusting. Naive. Then I end up getting walloped. *(He recalls)* Went downhill faster than a snowball, didn't I, eh? Zombie. Sitting around moping, drinking too much...no wonder I ended up with gallstones. Don't know what I'd have done without you and Sylvie, but...
[LORNA: *(Mimics him)* 'It was old Doctor Meadows did it...'
OLLIE: ...it was old Doctor Meadows did it. Telling me to take up an interest, something quiet, relaxing. The Chess Club—took to it like a duck to whatsit. Wonder what your Mum would say if she knew I was the local chess champ. Me, old bonehead Ollie. She used to say I was a slob. She may have had a point. But I'm a slob with an aptitude now. Strange, discovering an aptitude. Like finding money in the pocket of an old coat. *(He finishes brushing his shoes.)* Sometimes you get the feeling that there really is Someone Up There. A fine woman, is Pam. Couldn't fit the bill better if I'd ordered her out of a catalogue.

OUR OWN KIND
by Roy MacGregor
England - Present - Steve (20)

Following an argument with his girlfriend, Steve gets very drunk and allows his friends to talk him into stabbing a man to death. Here, Steve panics when he realizes what he has done.

STEVE: *(Ranting)* Shit. Oh shit. Shit, shit...shit! Must have been mad. Insane! Nah...pissed. Pissed and pilled. Pissed and pilled, out of it. S'what it was. Shit! It's all over. Finito. 'Fore I've even got started. Finished...'cos of a moment of madness. That's all it was, Your Honour, a moment of fuckin' madness! Insanity on legs! And now I'm binned. Binned. Oh shit oh fuckin' shit. *(He drops to his knees.)* Scared. Bloody scared. Fuckin' bowels dissolving. Don't want to be banged-up. Too young, too pissin' young. Ain't got the nick mentality. Banged-up with a load of psychos and arse-peddlers. Binned. Twenty-three hours a day, no sunlight 'cept what comes through prison bars. Too young, too fuckin' young. It's not fair! *(He makes a decision, leaps to his feet.)* End it. That's the answer. End it. Ain't no prison bird. Not me. Go mad. Mental. End it. Now. *(Daines enters. He is forty-ish. He lingers as if taking the air, but his expression is sour. Steve is unaware of his presence, takes a football scarf from his belt and loops it around his neck like a noose.)* Point of principle. Top 'em. String 'em up. Let 'em dangle. Principle—top the fuckers! I'll be a legend, a fuckin' folk hero! They'll be talking about it for the next fifty years. That old Steve...that Stevie boy...had class, had style, bottle. The man they couldn't bin. A legend! Went out like a champion! England's finest! They'll write songs about me! I'll be immortal! *(His face drops.)* I'll be dead. What good's being immortal if you're fuckin' dead?

OUT THE WINDOW
by Neal Bell
A farm by the sea - Present - Jake (30's)

Following a night of revelry, Jake and Andrea find themselves
magically transported to a beautiful old farm by the sea from
their apartment in New York City. Jake has experienced his
first orgasm in years and finds himself filled with emotion.
Here, he recalls their lovemaking.

JAKE: I remember how we got here.
[ANDY: How?]
JAKE: You were sitting on me, you were bending over to brush my
face with your hair, and I all of a sudden knew, if you moved again,
I was going to shoot, for the very first time since I hurt myself, a lot
of years in the desert and rain at last, like a gift I'd given up asking
for, and you started to move and I grabbed your ass, to hold the
moment before I came, know I was going to be released and feel it
all about to come down, this wind before a thunderstorm, you were
licking my lips, I was holding you still, and holding you still, and
just then...right then...we were standing beside each other, *standing*,
holding hands, in this milky light getting lighter, in Great Uncle
Somebody's yard...Uncle *Norbert*...god, Uncle Norbert...and we
started to run down the hill, that's what we'd do, back then, run
down this hill to the water's edge...and the hill was so steep, you'd
hit a place where you knew you couldn't stop anymore, if you tried
you'd fall, so you'd just keep running, faster and faster, trying to
move your legs as fast as the rest of your body was falling, you'd
hear this roar in your ears, and the light on the water would blind
your eyes, and all you'd want to do was run on forever.

THE RABBIT FOOT
by Leslie Lee
Rural Mississippi - 1920 - Johnny Hopper (20-30)

A bluesman with a traveling minstrel show, Johnny Hopper finds himself in one scrape after another. During a calm moment in between shows and confrontations, Johnny shares the following story of his first encounter with a harmonica.

JOHNNY HOPPER: Mean old thing. Used to sit on his porch playin' on his harmonica. Man could play a harmonica! I used to go over all the time to his front porch and sit on the steps and watch him, just a-wishin' I could play and he knows it. But he ain't gonna teach me nothin' cause he's so damn evil. He could do a train whistle, like this, Singin' Willie. *(HE imitates a train whistle on the harmonica.)* And then, he'd look at me with this grin on his face, and he'd say, "I bet you'd like to blow a train whistle like that, wouldn't you?" And then, the sonabitch'd go right on playin'. Evil, I'm tellin' you. But, you see, I kept on watchin' 'im. And one day, I got old 'nough, I buy me my own harmonica. Man, Singin' Willie, I was happier than a fly on watermelon. And first thing, I start practicin' my train whistles. I go down to the train track, and I wait for the trains, and I listen to 'em, 'cause all them engineers got a different way a blowin'. And I'd practice. And finally, one day, I learned it good. Real good! And that's when I goes over to Peabody's porch. And he's says, "Where you been, son, I ain't seen you in a bit?" Well, I don't say nothin' I just start blowin' train whistles. *(HE plays the harmonica with gusto.)* Man, Singin' Willie, I played all kindsa train whistles. My train was whistlin' from Memphis to Texas. My train was all over the Yew-nited States. I stood on that porch right in front a him, and I played 'til sweat was 'pourin' down my face—*(Demonstrates.)* I played 'til I thought my brains was gonna fly out. I played 'til that 'ol' man picked up his harmonica and started to blow—*(Blowing.)* and I blew. *(HE plays, going wild.)* Finally, neither one a us could blow no more. Too tired. Lips was raw and heads was achin'. And folks called it a draw.

58

THE RABBIT FOOT

(HOLLY DAY and BERTHA begin singin.)

JOHNNY HOPPER: But John Peabody knew who won it. I did, 'cause I learned that thing myself, with no help from nobody, and I ended up as good as him. I won it all right.

THE RABBIT FOOT
by Leslie Lee
Rural Mississippi - 1920 - Reggie (20's)

Reggie is a young black man whose life has been changed by his experiences in France in World War I. Here, Reggie tells his wife a story about a fellow soldier.

REGGIE: *(Moves away from her, trembling.)* I'd rather be in the ground than to live this way. *(Beat.)* There was this boy over there. His name was David Frames. We called him Little David. He said he was seventeen, but he probably lied 'bout his age. Might've been fifteen. From Arkansas. One night, I'm comin' back from guard duty. And it's cold and dark, and all I can hear is my feet crunchin' on the ice. All a sudden I hear somebody snifflin' and cryin'. And I gets close, and there's Little David, sittin' in the cold on some tree stump, huddled up to keep warm, and cryin' his fool head off. And he sees me, but it's too late to pretend he ain't cryin'. I done caught him! "What's wrong, Little David? You done got bad news from home?" He wouldn't tell me. And I says, "Come on, Little David you's a soldier in the Yew-nited States Army, and you ain't s'pposed to be cryin'. S'ppose some German soldier sneak up on you and see you cryin'? They'll swear they done got the war won." And finally he tells me. He's cryin' cause he's happy and sad at the same time. He's happy to be alive for the first time in his life, but he's scared to death a gettin' kilt by some German bullet. Just like ev'rybody else he found out what it is to be a man. And he kept talkin' bout goin' over the hill. He's gonna desert. He ain't gonna get kilt just when he knows what livin's 'bout. And I say, "Little David, you can't, man. Ain't no way. You're a colored man. And even if you do get a bullet, least you know what it's like to be treated like you s'pposed to." Anyway, he didn't run. He stayed. Well a bullet did get him one day near the end a the war. Blam! He didn't even know what hit 'im. Little David was gone. And that's what it was all about. Wasn't white women, it was Little David and Kansas City Jimmy and New York

60

THE RABBIT FOOT

Billy. All of 'em— gone! Done tasted a little bit a freedom, but a little bit's better n' nothin'. You all understand what I'm sayin'?

A RENDEZVOUS WITH GOD
by Miriam Hoffman
Here and Now - Itsik Manger (50+)

At the end of his life, the poet remembers the moment of his birth.

ITSIK MANGER:
One pair of shoes, one shirt to my name. What more do I need?
I can take off my shoes—I shall take off my shoes
I shall take off my shirt. What else do you want?
Is that how you want me to come back to you?
I'll come back to you as I am—A loser
A loser—A Loser—A Boozer—a chooser
Oh God, I'll never get it right.

I have a rendezvous with God, I shouldn't keep Him waiting.
He comes to me in my dreams and says:
"Enough Itsik, my vagabond poet. It's time you stopped dragging
your restless soul around the world."
So l say to Him:
"Deal God! How right you are! How right you are!
But there's so much I haven't done. There's one more song to be
written, and I haven't truly seen Jerusalem. And above all—
There's a brand new bottle of wine that I haven't finished yet—So
you see God
You'll have to wait awhile."
So He says to me:
"You can finish your song up here, and if you want to see
Jerusalem—From my side, you'll
have a heavenly view. And about that bottle of wine...
Bring it along and we'll both make a L'khayim."

He looks at me and smiles, the One Above.
He talks to me softly and lovingly:
"Come Itsikl! Come! I'm waiting for you with open arms.

A RENDEZVOUS WITH GOD

All of paradise can be yours forever"

Not so fast Gotenyu! Not so fast!
Before I submit to your divine embrace, I want you to know what
it was like to be a
Yiddish poet on this side of Paradise.
You wouldn't believe it
In the first place—Don't forget, Father in Heaven
That it wasn't my idea to be born.
It was my mother all along
Praying and pleading and insisting
That I must be born

I didn't come gently into this world, oh no...
I fought and I struggled and I caused her great pain.
She wept and she shrieked, and cursed my poor father:

"Oy...Murderer! Robber! It's all your fault! Do something!"

My father, pale and frightened, stood in the corner and said:

"Eh...eh...What can I do?"

Shoshe-Dvoshe, the midwife, tried every trick in the trade to
entice me into making an appearance:

"Nu! So come on out Itsikl!
I'll buy you a gold watch, a football, anything you 'mamzer'!
Shoshe-Dvoshe realized that I wasn't taking this birth very
seriously, so she turned to
my mother and said:
"Who does he think he is? Call me when he's ready."

And I laughed in her face and refused to be born

63

A RENDEZVOUS WITH GOD

It was friday night
My father gave up and went to the synagogue

My mother was left alone exhausted
The sight of her moved me deeply
After all I thought, a mother is a mother
But still, I refused to be born

The Sabbath candles flickered in every Jewish home, but our
     house stood dark and dreary
When all at once my mother stood up

"No! The Sabbath cannot be forsaken."

She lit the Sabbath candles, her hands over the flames
She covered her face and she whispered a prayer
This gentle vision touched my heart
Then and there I decided to be born

I stole my way out and hid behind her
I was born so quietly that my mother didn't even hear me
And I waited for her to stop praying
Each second seemed like a whole year
My heart was pounding like a frightened bird
Finally I could no longer contain myself
And I shouted out:
"Gut Shabbes mameh!"

Her eyes lit up, her face all aglow
She took me into her arms, she cuddled and caressed me and
kissed every little bone in
my body
She called me:
"Mayn malekhl! My Angel!

A RENDEZVOUS WITH GOD

Mayn oytser! My treasure!
Mayn likhtiker kadish!"

And I looked into her loving eyes, into her lovely face
And I knew that her love would bind me forever

SALAAM, HUEY NEWTON, SALAAM
by Ed Bullins
Street corner in W. Oakland - Present - Marvin (40-50)

Here, an acquaintance of Dr. Huey Newton describes his descent into the horrific world of crack cocaine.

MARVIN: In 1984 I became addicted to crack cocaine....Many people, especially members of my family, found my addiction difficult to understand. "You're so strong," they would say. "How could you become a weak, pitiful dope fiend?" But I did....My addiction came in my fortieth year, for many people, a time of disillusionment with life, and certainly it was for me....I was burnt out....Tired of revolution, tired of family life, sex and women, tired of working in the educational system, tired of the black middle class and the grass roots, tired of religious sectarianism, Christian and Muslim alike, tired....

Maybe this is what happens when one lives too fast. You not only get burned out, but you run out of ideas....What mountain shall I conquer next?....And a voice came to me and said: "You shall become Sisyphus. You shall roll a rock up a mountain and it shall fall to earth, and you shall begin again each day for eternity, since you can't figure out anything else to do, you big dummy!"

So I was a sitting duck for an addiction, that is, a new addiction, especially when I became an entrepreneur and had large sums of cash on a daily basis. Yeah, I sold incense and perfume oils and lots of stuff on the street at Market and Powell in San Francisco. I made a lot of quick, easy money....And money added to my problems because I hated making money. I actually felt guilty about it and had to do something with all that money I had....So my friends, including my so-called Muslim brothers, introduced me to crack....I didn't like sniffing cocaine. For one reason, my mind is naturally speedy, so I did not want anything to speed it up more. I wanted to slow down, relax. My thing was weed. I admit, I abused weed because I smoked it from morning 'til night for over twenty years....My thing was weed, wine and women. I always said I

66

SALAAM, HUEY NEWTON, SALAAM

wanted to die from an overdose of weed, wine and women, but along came crack and soon I had no desire for wine, weed or women. With all my knowledge, I had forgotten the simple rules of life: for every blues, there is a happy song—sing a happy song—it takes the same energy as the blues....Even before my addiction to crack, why couldn't I think of all the good in my life? Why couldn't I sing songs of praise to Allah, my God, for the beautiful parents He had blessed me with, for my beautiful brothers and sisters, for the beautiful, intelligent women I had had, for the most beautiful children any man could imagine? Why? Why? Why?....Yes, I know now....because I thought I was self-sufficient.

I had sat and watched my friends smoking crack, but at first it didn't interest me. I did not like the way they behaved....I'd come into the room and they wouldn't even look up and acknowledge my presence. They were all staring at whoever had the pipe....But finally, the devil caught me, only because I forgot Allah.

(HE chants.)

> I lost my wife behind the pipe
> I lost my children
> behind the pipe
> I lost my money
> behind the pipe
> I lost my mind
> behind the pipe
> I lost my life
> behind the pipe...

Yes, crack sent me to the mental hospital four times....Many times I put crack on my pipe and took that big 747 hit, and I could feel death coming, could feel my body surrounded by the strangest sensation. I would run to the window for air, or run outside for air. But after the moment of death had passed, I returned to my room and continued smoking....Once I accidentally cut my wrist, cut an artery. I dropped one of my pipes and grabbed at the broken pieces, cutting me critically, but I was unaware. I thought the bleeding would stop, but it didn't. I found my backup pipe and fired up....A friend tried to get me to go to the hospital, but I thought the blood would stop dripping from my wrist. It didn't. My new pipe became covered with blood. My dope had turned the color of blood. My clothes, the rug, the bed, the curtain, were all covered with blood. But I didn't stop. I kept on smoking....Finally, my friend got the hotel manager and he came in with a baseball bat and forced me out of the room....The paramedics came and took me to the hospital.... Ha ha ha....after the emergency room crew stitched my wound, I got on the bus and returned to my room to finish smoking....Hell, I still had sixty bucks....fuck it!

SOUTHERN CROSS
by Jon Klein
Rural Southern United States - 1850 - Captain (30-60)

Here, a seasoned navigator of the Mississippi spins an unbelievable yarn about alligators.

CAPTAIN: Welcome aboard. *(The Captain stops and scans the audience, as if someone asked him a question.)* What's that? Somebody got a question for the Captain?...Allygators? What you wanna know 'bout them for?...Oh I see. So you heard you might see a few gators on this trip, did ya. *(Pause. He scratches his head.)* Well now. I guess I've seen my share o' gators in my time. Don't think I better tell you bout 'em, though. Cause you'd think I was lyin' to you, and that's somethin' I never do. I kin cheat at cards, drink whiskey or chaw terbacker, but I jest can't bring myself to tell a lie. I guess it's a point of pride with certain men. *(Pause.)* You know, one time I counted eleven hundred gators to the mile from Vicksburg clear down to Orleans. And one time I seen three thousand four hundred and fifty-nine of them sittin' on one sandbar. I know it sounds like a lot, but I had a government surveyor aboard, and he checked 'em off as I counted. *(Pause.)* Yep. This used to be a reg'lar paradise for allygators. They were so thick that the sternwheel killed an average of forty-nine to the mile. True as the Gospel. Almost felt sorry for the cussed beasts, I killed so many. I sailed with one captain, name o' Captain Tom, always carried a thousand bottles o' liniment just to throw to the wounded ones. And as the gators got to know his boat, they'd swim and rub their tails against the boat, and purr like cats. One day he grounded on a sandbar, and the gators gathered round, got under the stern, and humped her clean over the bar by a grand push. Solemn truth. And when Captain Tom was dead, and the news got along the river, every gator in the river daubed his left ear with black mud as a badge of mournin', and several of 'em pined away and died in the sorrow. Now I know that sounds like a big story, but I never tole a lie yet, and never will. I wouldn't lie for all the money you could put on this boat. *(Long pause.)* My engines gave out once. A crowd of gators took a tow line and hauled us forty-five miles upstream to Vicksburg.

SOUTHERN CROSS
by Jon Klein
Rural South - 1912 - Huey P. Long (19)

Huey reveals his ambition to a travelling salesman who has discovered him hungry and cold in an old railroad shack.

LONG: Followed the railroad tracks from Oklahoma City.
[JACKSON: You're saying you walked here? That's eighteen miles.]
LONG: Ain't nothin' darker or colder than walkin' the rails at night. I heard voices, mister. Laughter. Animals. Faces grinnin' at me like jackals. I swear to you now mister, to you and God and anyone else who gives a damn, that I will never be poorer than I am on this January night in 1912. I've come to understand the power of a dollar in this country. The rich have all the power and they use it to keep down the poor. Well I'm gonna have me some of that power, only I'm gonna use it against the rich. They won't forget the day Huey P. Long stood up to them.

SOUTHERN CROSS
by Jon Klein
Rural South - 1850 - Captain (30-60)

Here, the Captain tells a tall tale about the biggest steamboat he ever saw.

CAPTAIN: All aboard that's goin' aboard. *(He turns to the audience.)* What's that? Why yes, it *is* a pretty good sized steamer, thank you. Ain't the biggest I ever seen, though. That honor would have to belong to the Jim Johnson. How big was it? Oh now, I don't think I should be tellin' you about the Jim Johnson. Cause you might take me for a liar, and most folks round here will vouch that I'm not one to profess falsehoods and untruths. No sir. Not me. *(Pause.)* Now I won't say exactly how big she was, but when the Jim Johnson passed by, the people used to stand on the riverbank and watch her from Easter Sunday to high noon on the Fourth of July. Yep, they had to put hinges on her every half mile or so, jest so she could make the turns in the river. The truth, as I live and breathe. And you talk about your big crews. Once the clerk tried to cut down expenses by not dotting the i's or crossing the t's on the pay checks. Saved himself a barrel of ink. Course there weren't any calendars on the Jim Johnson, since you could never pin down a single day we would arrive at any one place. The only way we knew when payday came around was to paint one paddle on the sternwheel white. It came up once a month. *(Pause.)* They had elevators up to the forty-second deck, and on the thirty-ninth deck they had the grand double-rush ballroom. Every pendant of glass in the chandeliers of that room was tipped with a fourteen-carat diamond. All you had to do was light one candle in that ballroom and all those diamonds blazed up like a bonfire. And they say that out on the hurricane deck it was wonderful, too. Young fellows walkin' round with their sweethearts under the magnolias. 'Course those days are gone forever now. *(Pause.)* Oh, I can see that look on your face. Well, if everything I've told you ain't the straight and narrow truth, may my tongue shrivel up and fall out o' my head.

SOUTHERN CROSS

(He waits a moment, testing fate.) All aboard! Gotta push off now. I'll catch up with you later. *(He starts off then turns back to the audience.)* By the way, the Jim Johnson had a one-mile race track round one o' the smokestacks. And a baseball park on top o' the pilot house.

SPARKY'S LAST DANCE
by Richard Lay
Prison in the South - Present - Hurricane (30)

On the eve of his electricution, Hurricane muses over his past.
Here, he fantasizes about entering the boxing ring one more
time.

HURRICANE: *(Day dreaming—delivered slowly.)* I'll stand in the
ring in red and gold dressing gown. It'll have ma name on the
back...*(Pause.)* Across the ring will be a black mother fucker.
(Intent.) The bell will ring and as if in slow motion I will take three
steps to the centre of the ring and hit him first—on the jaw. He will
reel back on to the ropes and I will step in and deliver the perfect
right upper-cut and follow-up...with a classic left hook. He will go
down on the ropes, his guard coming out of his mouth like a baby's
pacifier...splashing across the ring like a demented jelly fish...
(Deliberately—each word.) The referee will send me to my corner
and I will watch with detachment as the time-keeper and the referee
count to ten...*(Excited.)* And then I will be champion and jump
twice in the air and pray to God...as my trainer and my seconds
move in and hoist me above their shoulders. I AM the champion of
the world. NBC will come into the ring and on camera I will thank
everybody from Lily to Jesus Christ...and answer questions about the
fight...and just like a slow-motion film, the one I have seen so many
times...I will go to the corner of my opponent and put my gloved
hand around his shoulder...*(Smiles.)* We are now blood brothers.
I have won and he is the ex-champion. A woman in the ring will
leap into my arms and hug and kiss me and I will go back to my
dressing room...and drink champagne.

THE SUBSTANCE OF FIRE
by Jon Robin Baitz
New York City - 1987 - Martin (30-40)

When Martin joins his father, brother, and sister to discuss the
future of the family publishing business, tempers flare and harsh
words are exchanged. Here, Martin reveals his reasons for not
caring what happens.

MARTIN: Poison! You want to talk about poison? Look at what
you've done. You've created a family of literary zombies. You
know that people are afraid of you. It's why you've gotten so far.
Yes. "Isaac Geldhart knows something, he came from some awful
childhood in Europe that nobody knows about." He has a "seer-like
standing in the book world." Blah-Blah-Blah— phooey. Let me tell
you, we're fucked up by it. I grew up running around this building.
When I was eight, you gave me the Iliad in Greek so that someday
I could read it. Monster! People's lives are ruined by books and
they're all you know how to relate to, Dad. You too, Aaron, for all
your talk. You too, Sarah, pretending you hate to read. Sometimes
I want to take a pruning shears and do an Oedipus on myself. I
counted my books last week. Do you know how many I have?
Want to take a guess? *(No one says anything)* Fourteen thousand,
three hundred, and eighty six. The sixty crates of books that mom
left me. Well, I finally had them carted up the Hudson, but I had to
have shelves built. The whole house. Every room. And instead of
just guessing—I was, I mean—speechless. A wreck of a life. It just
flashed before my eyes. No sex, no people, just books 'til I die.
Dickens. In *French*. The bastard didn't write in French. What the
fuck am I doing with "Dombey and Son" in French? The twelve-
volume "Conquest of Mexico." Two hundred cookbooks. The
"Oxford World Classics," the little ones with the blue bindings, you
know?

[ISAAC: You got that?]

75

THE SUBSTANCE OF FIRE

MARTIN: They're all just words. And this is life, and besides, I hear the book chains are now selling pre-emptive strike video games, so why bother anyway? I'm out.

[ISAAC: But really, there are limits, sweetheart.]

MARTIN: Yes. That's exactly right. There are limits. I believe I know that. Hey, I spent most of my sixteenth year getting chemotherapy, remember? And it's not that long ago, I can still feel it. I cannot waste my life. I feel you people dragging me into this thing. You want this confrontation, Dad. You want nothing more than your children gathered around you, fighting. Well forget it. You don't know what I feel in my back, in my bones. I wake up some days and I'm crying. I think I'm still at Sloan-Kettering, lying there hairless and white and filling up with glucose from a drip. Hey! I can't get that time back. I feel all the needles, some days, my lymph nodes, and I'm sweating. And part of my life is spent in fear, waiting. I know none of us has forever, know that very well, and I care very much how I spend my time. And involved in an internecine war over a publishing house, is, by my reckoning, Father, a dead waste. *And* if I choose to live with plants as an assistant lecturer at an over-rated seven-sisters school, *that* is my goddamn choice.

THE SUBSTANCE OF FIRE
by Jon Robin Baitz
New York City - 1987 - Isaac Geldhart (60's)

Isaac Geldhart is blamed by his son Aaron for the declining fortunes of the family publishing house. Aaron threatens to remove Isaac from the presidency with the support of his siblings, Martin and Sarah. However, when Sarah says she will support Isaac, he then has the controlling shares and he speaks to Aaron.

ISAAC: I spent a couple of days, a little boy, wandering around after the liberation. I saw a particular kind of man—a wraith-like figure—who could only have been in the camps. But with a brown pinstripe suit, a fleur-de-lis on his tie and manicured nails, trying to pick up where he left off, as if you could. I never say anything about this. Why talk? Why bother? I wasn't in the camps. I was in a basement. You know? They're busy throwing the Farbers and the Hirsches into the ovens, and I'm happily eating smoked eels in the basement, with my Stendahl and Dumas. What did I know? I was protected, sheltered by my cousins. And then I got out of the basement and into the wretched world. I came to this country. You re-invent yourself. Make it as a bon-vivant in Manhattan. Meet this woman—this extraordinary woman. Marry. Have these kids. Go to so many cocktail parties, host so many more...and they...haunt. *(Beat.)* I have kept my eyes closed to the world outside the basement for so long. The wrecked world all around us. But I can no longer close my eyes. *(HE turns to AARON.)* My son. You are fired. I will give you a week to clear your desk, and I will give you letters of recommendation. But I will not speak to you, I will not communicate with you, I will not...*(Pause.)...give at all.* Kiddo. To the victor go the spoils.

THE SUMMER THEY STOPPED MAKING LUDES
or How Taking Peyote Turned Me Into A Coyote
by Steven Tanenbaum
Poolside, suburbia - 1970's - Casey (17-20)

Here, Casey—who is flunking our of college—shares a joint and some sociological observations with his friend, Art.

CASEY: You should stop reading those Castaneda books. They're warping your mind.

[ART: I become a coyote so I can travel through the crack that separates the two worlds.]

CASEY: Art, didn't anybody leave you a wake-up call. This is the seventies not the sixties. And why you'd want to get stuck in that decade, I'll never know. I mean when I was a kid, I couldn't wait to grow up so I could go down to the malt shop, drop a dime in the juke box and slow dance to the Shirelles with Betty and Veronica. But the sixties blew all that shit off the map. Okay, so I adjusted my sights. You know, free love and fighting the good fight looks pretty good, too. Like every night there was some revolutionary on the Walter Cronkite Show saying fuck you to the system. Here's Malcolm X saying fuck you to whitey; and over there, Abble Hoffman's saying fuck you to Mayor Daley; and look it that, Muhammed Ali is saying fuck you to the draft board; and back on campus all the students are saying fuck you to the war, the pentagon and the president; and everybody, everywhere is saying fuck you to the monolithic, mayonnaise mentality. By now I'm pretty revved up to join the chorus; and so what happens when my time comes—Zap, the sixties disappear. Sorry, no more love-ins but you can't go back to Donna Reed, either, because she's long gone. Which pretty much leaves me with one option...Fuck you Abbie Hoffman; fuck you Richard Nixon; fuck you Martin Luther King; and fuck you Donovan.

78

TALKING THINGS OVER WITH CHEKHOV
by John Ford Noonan
Riverside Park, NYC - Present - Jeremy (40's)

When Jeremy bumps into Marlene, his ex, in the park, he gives her a copy of his new play to read. When next they meet to discuss his work, Jeremy reveals his fantasy relation- ship with Anton Chekhov and the stabilizing effect it has on his life.

JEREMY: Thank God for Chekhov. He's the only one who can calm me down. After I left you yesterday, I stopped for one drink each at all these different bars. Only works me up more. Get home at 5, flip on *Six Million Dollar Man*. At 6 I switch to 11 for *The Jeffersons* and *Barney Miller*. At 7 back to 5 for *Mash*. I'm exploding. I throw on my sweats. Seventeen times around the block. Up my five flights three and four steps at a time. I swing open my door. Flop to the floor for a set of push-ups. I notice his foot. Stop. Look up. He's sitting in my favorite rocker. Beautiful white linen suit. Felt hat. Walking cane. In his hand a bottle of something Russian. "Like some kvass?" "What's kvass?" He smiles. Pours me half a glass. He toasts, "To you!" "Why me?" "Tomorrow you'll be hearing what people think of your first play." He continues. This visit he's speaking Russian but somehow I hear it in English. "Plays make your life no longer your own. With stories you write it, mail it, good-by. But plays! Rehearsals. Production meetings. Picking the actors." Suddenly he seems about to go on and on. More kvass. He laughs and says, "I don't mind my characters when they go on and on, but I hate to do it myself. How about more kvass?" Another half glass. Now I'm tipsy too. "Close Friend," he mumbles, "you and I are alike in a very big way. We're afraid to let go. We're both way too serious." I smile. He smiles. Now I know why he keeps coming back. He almost drops the bottle and chuckles, "From a tipsy Russian take some silly advice: "ANY NUMBER OF PEOPLE CAN BE LUCKY ENOUGH TO WRITE ONE GOOD PLAY, BUT ONLY A FEW OF US ARE SMART ENOUGH TO DRESS LIKE WE'RE CAPABLE OF WRITING

TALKING THINGS OVER WITH CHEKHOV

MANY!" Chekhov laughs. I laugh. No two writers have ever howled louder. He goes on, "It's not only how you dress. It's any little thing that makes business easier. The right pencils. Paper you love to touch. A chair to work in that makes your back never hurt. Your desk in front of a window you love to look out of." He grabs my hand so tight I yelp. "CLOSE FRIEND, CONCENTRATE ON THE LITTLE THINGS. THEY'RE THE ONLY THINGS THAT ADD UP." He gets up, flips open the door with his walking cane and wobbles off.

TALKING THINGS OVER WITH CHEKHOV
by John Ford Noonan
New York City - Present - Jeremy (40's)

Jeremy and his ex, who is an ex-actress, have met jogging in the park and some old feelings have surfaced. He asks her to read a play he has written and she finds that the play is about them. She wants to talk to him about playing herself when the play is produced. Here, Jeremy explains why he wrote it.

JEREMY: *(Screaming.)* SIT!!
[MARLENE: *(Sitting next to Jeremy.)* Breathe deep. You forget to breathe deep when you're angry.]
JEREMY: [*(Even louder scream.)* MY MOTHER'S DEAD! STOP!] *(Pause.)* I wrote this play because I hated you so much. When we first split up, I dated a lot. Everyone I went out with brought you back. A gesture, a smile, a way of holding a cigarette. I gave up dating. Next, every woman I passed on the street became you. I avoided restaurants. I wouldn't board a bus. More and more I spent my days at home. Every night a different movie. Hours browsing in bookstores. One Thursday late I saw a book about Chckhov with his picture on the cover. I bought it. Took it home. Sat it on the desk. Stared at it. His mouth on the cover spoke, "THE MORE YOU HATE, THE LESS YOU REMEMBER!" I grabbed a piece of blank paper. Wrote down a sentence, "IN ANOTHER MINUTE I WAS GOING TO CALL THE COPS." I went to bed. Couldn't sleep. Jumped up. Wrote the next four lines. Thought I saw Chekhov on the cover smile. Then it hit me. That's what writing's about: the real remembering! By dawn I had the whole first scene copied. I read it. It wasn't great, but I saw what I had done. I had taken the resentments and revenges and hates I held against you and I had stripped them back. What I had found was sadness and hurt and under that the real you. I had gotten back to what was there when we first met. I had dug up the forgotten you, the Marlene I had cared about and trusted. I think that's a great lesson for both of us, don't you?

TALKING THINGS OVER WITH CHEKHOV

[MARLENE. What?]
JEREMY: THE MORE YOU HATE, THE LESS YOU REMEM-
BER.

UNCHANGING LOVE
by Romulus Linney
Manard, North Carolina - 1920's - Shelby (28)

Shelby, uneducated and crude, is drunk at his wedding and
boasts of his important connections and bright financial future.
Actually, he is being set up to take the fall for dishonest
politicians.

SHELBY: Yeah. Well, maybe. If I don't get asked more than
once. *(Pause.)* But let me tell you this. *(He looks about, very
drunk.)* Ain't no joke, neither. Old Ray Hobbs, who just might be
Lieutenant Governor of this here whole state, was in a real fix. Put
hisn in the wrong place, God Amighty, and who had to pull it out
for him? I did! That's when we got thick, me and Ray. That's
when my fortunes commenced to RISE, I mean, in the Capitol of
this State. I mean, he said, "Shelby, you have come to my attention.
I got my eye on you, boy! You're a natural born Sherlock God
damn Holmes, Buddy, and I got use for you." And he *has* use for
me. I am learning what enterprise can be! *(He falls, sprawling.
Judy reaches for him. He brushes her away, sits up.)* Yeah, I'm
knee-walking drunk! All right! *(He looks around.)* People think
I'm just good looking and stupid, but I ain't. In the ancient world,
Julius Caesar had to cross the Rub-i-con. That was a river. He
looked hard and clear, seen his chance and had the gumption to take
it, and he crossed that river, and won—well—some country or other.
Point is, he done it! He made his move!! I can, too!! Ray Hobbs
knows that, and he don't want no dollar tomorrow neither, Daddy.
He wants his dollar today! So do I, just like you. Just like you.
(He staggers to his feet.) And I'll tell ye this here. Making that
kind of money, that's what'll separate the men from the boys. *(He
stares at Judy.)* I jest got married, didn't I? I'm a safe and
substantial citizen. So where are these old wimmen to say goodbye
to?

VEINS AND THUMBTACKS
by Jonathan Marc Sherman
New Jersey - Present - Jimmy Bonaparte (28)

All his life, Jimmy has dreamed of something greater than his life as a supermarket stock boy. After nearly 10 years of playing amateur nights at a local comedy club, The Laugh Riot, Jimmy's frustration is reaching a critical point. When his quarrelsome old grandmother falls ill, his fear and anxiety of losing her permeate his act.

JIMMY: Pleasure to be here at the Laugh Riot's bi-weekly amateur night. I'm Jimmy Bonaparte, and ice cream runs through my veins. My sixth grade teacher told me that and I've never been able to forget it, especially since every time I get a paper cut, something pink that tastes like strawberry comes out instead of blood. I've been opening with that for—a long time. Strawberry paper cut. Umm, *hmm*. Well. Uhh, I've got—I have a television show, I don't know, some of you may have seen it, it's on channel thirty-one. Thursday night at eleven-thirty. It's called "The American Dream," uhh, and I just, I don't know, call me fucking crazy, I felt like plugging my own show up here, what *am* I? *Huh?* Uhh, so, uhh, *jokes*, on with the—the *funny*—the *jokes*. Uhh. Well, the other day, I stuck my tongue into the dollar bill space on a change machine, you know how it is when you see a really, uhh, good looking change machine, you start to French kiss it a little, and, uhh, all of a sudden my tongue was gone, or at least I thought it was, and I was fucking *terrified*, right, because I like my tongue. That's not funny. *(Pause)* I can't make you people laugh, not even if I wanted to, which, well, really I kind of *don't*, but even if I *did*, you know? Nobody here ever *laughs*. I'm the Goddamn American Dream! But nobody ever laughs. Why do you people come? You never *laugh*. So I *pay* to have a t.v. show, and nobody gives a flying fuck about that either. *(Pause)* A Flying Fuck. *What* an image. With parachutes or something. "Don't come till we're *about* to hit the ground, Honey." Ha, ha. That's not *funny!* *(Pause)* I just put my grandmother into the

84

VEINS AND THUMBTACKS

fucking hospital—I just put my grandmother into the hospital to die, you know, 'cause that's what grandmothers *do* in hospitals, it's what they *do*—grandmothers *die* in hospitals, that's what they *do*. *She's* gonna die. And I can't make you fucking *laugh*. I mean, you know, I took my little girl to the hospital to see my Grandma, her Great-Grandma, and it's a really fucking scary place, the hospital, and she didn't flinch a second, she just made her way straight to the old lady and looked at her and there was—such *goodness*. *Fuck*. What *happens*? *Where* does the bad shit start *happening*? *(Pause)* When I was young, I'd wait at my Grandma's bedside for her to wake up, holding a frying pan for scrambled eggs in one hand and a book by Dr. Seuss in the other hand. *Yertle The Turtle*. Great book. Every morning. Same book. Same frying pan. Same pajamas. Grandma never understood why I kept asking her to read the same book over and over—I think she got a little annoyed with me. She wasn't—she *isn't*, pardon me—she isn't a very *delicate* soul. "What is it about the book?" she'd want to know, but it wasn't anything about the book, it was her *reading* the book, and that feeling, knowing how she'd read it, that made me happy. *(Pause)* I forget when Grandma stopped reading that book to me. I don't even know where the stupid book *is*. It's probably in the basement. Along with everything else. Right? *(Pause) Right? (Pause)* *RIGHT?*

(The Nurse walks in, pushing the empty wheelchair. She turns it and leaves it. Jimmy looks at it.)

JIMMY: *(Beat)* No more jokes tonight. But if you want to laugh, go ahead.

WALKING THE DEAD
by Keith Curran
Boston - Present - Chess (30's)

Here, a troubled man shares the story of his parents' double
suicide and his subsequent struggle to cope with the loss.

CHESS: My parents committed suicide. I found them. I was 10
years old. I've put together the story, and here it is. Three months
before they killed themselves my parents went on diets. There was
quite a lot of nervousness in my family, and they went on diets. My
father was thin and his diet was to eat bread and pancakes and butter
and milkshakes. My mother was heavy and her diet was to eat
carrots. I ate what my father ate, but halfway through a meal he'd
look at my plate and say: "You done with that, son?" This was the
happiest time of my childhood because my parents were calm and
loved each other a whole lot. Then one day I came home from
school and the house was empty. I decided to get my racquet and
hit a few balls. I found them in the garage hanging from a support
beam. They were hanging from either end of the same rope, and
near their dangling feet were the chairs they'd kicked away. I
realise now that my parents went on their diets so they'd weigh the
same. I don't remember what I did after I found them, but I ended
up living with my Aunt Peg and going to a psychiatrist twice a
week. My Aunt Peg bought me a dog to make up for my loss, and
I tied a rope around the dog's neck, threw the rope up over a beam
in the downstairs family room, stood on a chair, and tied the other
end around my neck. I guess it's good I didn't have a younger
brother or sister. So I kicked the chair away and something cracked
and I hit the floor and something landed on the dog's head. It was
a fake beam just glued to the ceiling. I sprained my ankle and the
dog got a cut on its nose. I washed out the cut and put a bandaid on
it and hugged the dog until Uncle Hank found us and called my psychiatrist. —He told him what I did—and that I'd named the dog
"Mom and Dad"—and my psychiatrist thought that was interesting.
But I just liked it when my Aunt Peg said: "go feed Mom and Dad."

WALKING THE DEAD

I never cried about my parents committing suicide. I figured that if their decision to be dead was the reason we had those happy three months together, it wasn't up to me to get upset about it, and that really got on my psychiatrist's nerves. He kept saying that it was perfectly normal to cry—but I think he just wanted me to break down in his office and make him feel effective. Six months after my parents committed suicide, Mom and Dad was hit by a car. He died three hours later. I cried and cried. I couldn't stop. My psychiatrist thought all the crying was wonderful and explained that I was using Mom and Dad's death as an excuse to mourn my parents. But he was wrong. It was just for Mom and Dad. I loved that dog. Thank you.

WALKING THE DEAD
by Keith Curran
Boston - Present - Bobby (30's)

Bobby is angry that his homosexuality is monitored by society's stereotypes, and says so.

BOBBY: Bobby. *Why* am I Bobby. Why is Veronica Homer? I was Robert most of my life. Then for a while I became "Max". "Max" had a certain masculine brevity that proved effective in the clone-popular "I'll lean against this brick and look at you like I hate you, now *fuck* me, Mary" late 1970's. Then came safe sex and I became "Bobby!" A younger name. A less anally-entered name. Do you have anything? Any Wine-thing?

[CHESS: I think so.]

(Chess gets wine from the fridge.)

BOBBY: I am, in case you are paying due attention, embodying a classic homosexual stereotype for you at this time. The "Self-loathing Alcoholic Queen". Stereotypes are true, Chester! I mean, where do the "compassionately encumbered" think stereotypes *come* from, for God's sake? Some kind of far-right think-tank at a trailer park in Oklahoma City? Do they think all the "Joe-Bobs" and "Slims" and "Jim-Bos" sit around *brainstorming*? "Uh...*I* know! Why don't we say that homosexual men...*lisp!* Yeah, Joe-Bob, let's say they lisp and worship over-emotional, victimised, yet unattractive girl singers!" I mean, *homos—do—lisp!* Not *all* but *enough*. And black men *will* wear almost anything on their heads. Jewish mothers *do* smother their beloved male offspring. And heterosexual men *do* spend most of their post-pubescence fantasizing about getting repeated blow-jobs from lesbian twin sisters in the back seat of a '57 *Buick!* Not *ALL*—but *ENOUGH!* Just enough. The first emotion *I* felt upon reaching the age of reason was the feeling that I was

WALKING THE DEAD

"different". I did not throw footballs appropriately. I went to college and had *sex* with people who threw footballs appropriately—by getting them very drunk—or so they *said*. The resultant guilt, however, encouraged my last attempt at heterosexuality, which upon *FAILING*, allowed me to "resign myself to my fate" and move to a major American urban center where I found many fellows who were into show tunes, and who, when looking at an attractive man with an attitude, said things like: "Now whom does she think *she* is?" Next came working out and wearing hardhats, followed by working out and wearing polo shirts, followed by staying *in* and wearing condoms. Now I am old—in gay years—I am clever, superior and acerbic—and I serve as a rite of passage for younger homosexuals who warm my hardened heart with their simplicity, kindness, *lack* of cynicism and wrinkle-free, worshipful eyes. Bing, bing, bing, bing, bing, and I can't *stand* it! I have been, and continue to be, every stereotype I loathe. I can't get *away* from it! What began with the terrifying realisation that I was "different" has been replaced by the even *more* terrifying realisation that I am the *same*.

WHITE CHAMELEON
by Christopher Hampton
Alexandria, Egypt - 1952-1956 - Christopher (16-17)

Christopher, living during a time of brutality and instability in the Egypt of the 1950's, tries to explain what it implies about the tides of life.

CHRISTOPHER: Alexandria. In 331 BC, Alexander the Great ordered its foundation on a crescent of land which lay open like a wound to the sea; and, eight years later, they brought him back in a glass coffin, so that he could see at last the city he had conjured into being. Over the next two centuries it became, under the incestuous Ptolemaic dynasty, the intellectual centre of the world. More than the Pharos lighthouse, the Great Library was one of the Seven Wonders. Euclid perfected his system of geometry here; Eratosthenes, working from the assumption that the earth was round, calculated its circumference to within 50 miles, while his colleague, Aristarchus, proposed that it revolved around the sun; the first systematic dissection of corpses allowed the Alexandrians to suggest that the blood circulated and that the brain was the seat of the intelligence; and the first grammar was compiled. Before long, most of this was forgotten again. *(There's a strange sound, like a burst of exquisite music, travelling across the sky. CHRISTOPHER looks up, waiting for it to pass.)* There is a legend that shortly before Mark Antony died, he heard a burst of exquisite music, travelling across the sky: this was the god Hercules, abandoning him to his fate. In a famous poem, Constantine Cavafy, who wrote in Greek and spent his life in Alexandria, alters the legend, so that it is Alexandria herself who is leaving Antony. In these circumstances, the poet advises stoicism and gratitude, not cowardice or guilt or self-deception: because sooner or later all of you must lose your Alexandria.

PERMISSIONS ACKNOWLEDGMENTS

Grateful acknowledgment is made for permission to reprint excerpts from the following plays:

ADVICE FROM A CATERPILLAR by Douglas Carter Beane. © Copyright, 1991, by Douglas Carter Beane. Reprinted by permission of the author and Graham Agency, New York. CAUTION: Professionals and amateurs are hereby warned that ADVICE FROM A CATERPILLAR is subject to a royalty. It is fully protected under the copyright laws of the United States of America, and of all countries covered by the International Copyright Union (including Canada and the rest of the British Commonwealth), and of all countries covered by the Pan-American Copyright Convention and the Universal Copyright Convention, and of all countries with which the United States has reciprocal copyright relations. All rights, including professional, amateur, motion picture, recitation, lecturing, public reading, radio broadcasting, television, audio and video recording, and the rights of translation into foreign languages are strictly reserved. All inquiries concerning professional or amateur performance rights should be addressed to Samuel French, Inc., 45 West 25th Street, New York, NY 10010. Inquiries concerning all other rights should be addressed to Graham Agency, 311 West 43rd Street, New York, NY 10035.

AL PACINO by Bryan Goluboff. © Copyright, 1990, by Bryan Goluboff. Reprinted by permission of the author's agent, George P. Lane, William Morris Agency, 1350 Avenue of the Americas, New York, NY 10019.

BABYLON GARDENS by Timothy Mason. © Copyright, 1991, by Timothy Mason. Reprinted by permission of the author's agent, Peter Franklin, William Morris Agency, 1350 Avenue of the Americas, New York, NY 10019.

THE BALCONY SCENE by Wil Calhoun. Copyright registration number PA 1322454 by Wil Calhoun. Reprinted by permission of the author.

BLACK EAGLES by Leslie Lee. © Copyright, 1991, by Leslie Lee. Reprinted by permission of the author's agent, Ellen Hyman, 422 East 81st Street, New York, NY 10028.

BLACKWATER by J. Dakota Powell. © Copyright, 1991, by J. Dakota Powell. Reprinted by permission of the author's agent. For a copy of the play, please send $5 and a SASE to Peregrine Whittlesey, 345 East 80th Street, New York, NY 10021.

BLOOD ISSUE by Harry Crews. © Copyright, 1991, by Harry Crews. Reprinted by permission of the author.

BODY AND SOUL by John Glines. © Copyright, 1991, by John Glines. Reprinted by permission of the author.

BREAKING UP by Michael Cristofer. © Copyright, 1991, by Michael Cristofer.

91

PERMISSIONS ACKNOWLEDGMENTS

amateur, motion picture, recitation, lecturing, public reading, radio and television broadcasting and the rights of translation into foreign languages are strictly reserved. Particular emphasis is laid on the question of readings, permission for which must be secured from the author's agent in writing. All inquiries concerning the amateur and professional production right to SALAAM, HUEY NEWTON, SALAAM should be addressed in writing to the author's agent, Helen Merrill, Ltd., 435 West 23rd Street, Suite 1A, New York, NY 10011, USA. No amateur performance of the play may be given without obtaining, in advance, the written permission of Helen Merrill, Ltd. All inquiries concerning rights (other than production rights) should be addressed to Helen Merrill, Ltd.

SOUTHERN CROSS by Jon Klein. © Copyright, 1991, by Jon Klein. CAUTION: SOUTHERN CROSS, being duly copyrighted is subject to a royalty. The stage performance rights (other than first class rights) are controlled exclusively by the Dramatists Play Service, Inc., 440 Park Avenue South, New York, NY 10016. No professional or non-professional performance of the play (excluding first class professional performance) may be given without obtaining in advance the written permission of the Dramatists Play Service, Inc., and paying the requisite fee. Inquiries concerning all other rights should be addressed to Lois Berman, 240 West 44th Street, New York, NY 10036.

SPARKY'S LAST DANCE by Richard Lay. © Copyright, 1991, by Richard Lay. Reprinted by permission of the author's agent, Robert Ganshaw, 244 West 74th Street, New York, NY 10023.

THE SUBSTANCE OF FIRE by Jon Robin Baitz. © Copyright, 1991, by Jon Robin Baitz. Reprinted by permission of the author's agent, George P. Lane, William Morris Agency, 1350 Avenue of the Americas, New York, NY 10019.

THE SUMMER THEY STOPPED MAKING LUDES or How Taking Peyote Turned Me Into A Coyote by Steven Tanenbaum. © Copyright, 1990, by Steven Tanenbaum. The play premiered April 16, 1991 and is still running at Dick Shea's Studios, New York City. Reprinted by permission of the author.

TALKING THINGS OVER WITH CHEKHOV by John Ford Noonan. © Copyright, 1991, by John Ford Noonan. Reprinted by permission of the author's agent, Don Buchwald and Associates, Inc., 10 East 44th Street, New York, NY 10017.

UNCHANGING LOVE by Romulus Linney. © Copyright, 1991, by Romulus Linney. CAUTION: UNCHANGING LOVE, being duly copyrighted is subject to a royalty. The stage performance rights (other than first class rights) are controlled exclusively by the Dramatists Play Service, Inc., 440 Park Avenue South, New York, NY 10016. No professional or non-professional performance of the play (excluding first class professional performance) may be given without obtaining in advance the written permission of the Dramatists Play Service, Inc., and paying the requisite fee. Inquiries concerning all other rights should be addressed to Peregrine Whittlesey, 345 East 80th Street, New York, NY 10021.

94